# Abandoned For Life

### The Incredible Story
### Of One Romanian Orphan
### Hidden From The World

### His life. His words.

by

## Izidor Ruckel

Joan Bramsch, Editor

Abandoned For Life
The Incredible Story of One Romanian Orphan
Hidden From The World. His life. His words.


Copyright © Izidor Ruckel 2002
          Joan Bramsch, Editor
All rights reserved
Publication Date: November, 2002
E-Book Copyright © November, 2002
ISBN 978-0-934334-13-6

E-Published simultaneously worldwide.

Published by:
**JB INFORMATION STATION**
Box 515165
St. Louis MO 63151
314-638-3404 (voice)
Email: romania@JoanBramsch.com
Web site: http://www.EmpoweredParent.com

ONLINE SALES:
http://www.joanbramsch.com/romania.html


### Legal Notices

No part of this manual, except for brief passages in articles and reviews that refer to author and publisher, may be reproduced or copied in any way or manner without written permission of the author. See contact above.

This book is not intended as a source of any advice such as medical or legal. The reader or purchaser assumes all responsibility for the use of this information. The author and publisher assume no responsibility or liability whatsoever on behalf of the purchaser or reader of this information.

## Dedication and Acknowledgments

**To My Family:**

This autobiography is dedicated to my Family -- Marlys, Daniel, Izabela, Jennifer, Robin and Cari Ruckel. I also dedicate this book to my biological brother, Mugurel Bojani.

**To My Friends:**

This autobiography is also dedicated to Maria Petreus, Maria Grigor Onisa, Dina Codrea, Ildi Strimbei, Emilia Duma, Marina Turda, Danna Pasca, Florica Arba, Anita Lingurar, Cardos Daniel and Tibi Varga.

Special Thanks:

I want to thank God and my Lord Jesus Christ for being in my life. It is only through God that we can accomplish anything in life and through Him that we might be born again.

Thanks to my family for being such an awesome family and for all that they did for me to be adopted. It is loving people like my parents and sisters who make a difference in other people's lives. Thanks to my family, I am well and alive today.

I owe a "standing" ovation and a great debt of gratitude to my surgeon Dr. Bernsten and his staff at the Shriners Hospital in San Diego, California. Their skill and training, and their dedication to children, provides a great role model for me as I, too, hope to help children. Thank you for helping me.

Thanks also to Janice Tomlin and Tom Jarriel of the *ABC News 20/20* organization for always remembering the ones left behind in Romanian orphanages and hospitals, and for all the stories about the orphans that they have shared with the world. One of the reasons so many more children were adopted after me was because of the efforts of both Janice Tomlin and John Upton. John rescued me from hell.

Thanks also to Maggie Ring, Daniel Ruckel and Diane Marten for helping me with my autobiography and for helping me put together special presentations on the Romanian orphans. Maggie Ring (http://www.juiceplus.com/+mr41049), and Daniel Ruckel, my Dad, were always there to support me at all my presentations and to help me compose my speeches.

I want to give special thanks to the Board of **Mount San Jacinto Community College**, whose members awarded me a full scholarship to attend classes, starting August 19, 2000. It is also important for me to thank two special persons at the college who continue to be instrumental in helping me make my dreams come true to become educated and to facilitate my plan to help my friends left behind in Romania. Thank you, Interim Dean of Instruction, Jan Noble, and thank you, Director of Public Information and Marketing, Bill Marchese.

Most of all, I would like to thank Joan Bramsch, founder of http://www.EmpoweredParent.com and a best-selling author, for being my editor, and for putting in all the hard effort that she has into this work. This autobiography was possible for publishing and for you to read, only because of Joan Bramsch and her staff.

In the future I plan to return to Romania. There are still so many more orphans to help. That's why this book must be a bestseller as an ebook and CD first, and then as a print book, because twenty-five percent of the profits will be used to provide shelter and education for the orphans of Romania.

**If you can open a door to funding, please mailto:romania@JoanBramsch.com**

I want to thank you for buying this book. All that I have written, every word, is the truth as I remember it. It is sometimes a sad story, but it is never hopeless because there are survivors from these hard times and *I am one!*

Sincerely,
**Izidor Ruckel**

**http://www.izidor.org**

ONLINE SALES:
http://www.joanbramsch.com/romania.html

http://www.hometown.aol.com/colindeizidor/myhomepage/business.html

**This web page is the transcription between 20/20 and Izidor, when he finds his biological family.**
http://sixtyminutes.ninemsn.com.au/60/stories/2001_11_04/story_471.asp

**This web site contains more information. Click on "20/20 Story."**
http://www.johnupton.net

http://www.cherishourchildren.org/programs/programs.asp

http://www.childrenintheson.com

http://www.abcnews.com

http://www.childrenoftheworld.org

~~~~~~~~~~~~~~~~~~~~~~~~~~~~~~~~~~~~

Dear Reader,

I am going to reprint here, the opening page of my web site - http://www.izidor.org - so you can get an overview of what you will read in my autobiography.

"Hello... my name is Izidor Ruckel.

In 1990 I was discovered by American Filmmaker John Upton in a terrible asylum, the **"Hospital for Irrecoverable Children,"** located in the northwest mountain town of *Sighetu Marmatiei, Romania*. I had been confined there most of my life because my birth parents abandoned me. John promised to find me a home in America. He videotaped me and showed the tape to some wonderful people, the Ruckel family in *San Diego, California*. They promised to adopt me. In 1991 I was adopted by Marlys and Daniel Ruckel, who have done Angel Work most of their lives. They saved me.

In 1994 my dream was to go back to Romania to see my homeland and visit my friends once again. Every day and every night, for years, I prayed that I would be allowed to return. By the grace of God my dream did come true when He finally answered my prayer.

This is how God worked his blessing for me:

*ABC News 20/20* flew me back to Romania on March 25, 2001 as part of their follow-up story on the series -- **THE SHAME OF A NATION**. 20/20 located my biological parents who had left me twenty years before at the hospital because I was crippled. I also got to meet my sisters and brothers. I didn't know I had siblings. I didn't know I had any relatives there. I continue to keep in touch with one of my brothers.

While in Romania, I went back to the hospital where I had been kept for eleven years. I saw many friends there, friends I grew up with, still in the same hospital, living under the same terrible conditions I'd left ten years before. It nearly broke my heart.

Some of my friends were not there and I had to find them. I discovered those "missing" friends had reached the age of 21 years and all had been transferred to the *Old Men's Home*. It was hard for me to see my young friends stuck in the *Hospital for Irrecoverable Children*, and the *Old Men's Home*. It was almost unbearable because I now live in America where I have much more opportunities and freedom then they would ever enjoy. Unless...

Once I returned to the United States I was determined to do whatever I could to help the Romanian children, barely existing in cruel orphanages, hospitals and geriatric homes, as well as, the children 20/20 had focused on, who live in the rat-infested, dank, dark and cold, unhealthy sewers and canals of the capital city.

Shortly after the first *ABC News 20/20 Special* program entitled **"Children For Sale,"** aired on June 8, 2001, I wanted to work with an organization that would work with me, as well. Now, armed with a recommendation from 20/20, I contacted a nonprofit group known as *Cherish Our Children International* founded in 1993, by Juli Kamin.

With help from my good friend Maggie Ring, I created a special presentation to raise money to help the Romanian orphans and abandoned children on the streets. My first presentation was held in San Jacinto, CA. It was so successful that I soon was invited to speak in Temecula CA. I discovered I could do this; I could influence others to help, simply by explaining the terrible need!

On February 23-27, 2002, *Cherish Our Children International* flew me to Houston, Texas and Chicago, Illinois, for a new presentation that was put together by Dana St. John, Carla Heiser, and many friends who volunteered their time to help. These talks too were successful. I look forward to finding new opportunities to speak on a need I believe I am called to help solve.

If you want me to come speak to your group,
you can reach me here:

**mailto:romania@joanbramsch.com Subject: IZIDOR**

To that end, I have written this autobiography. With the help of my editor, Joan Bramsch, the story covers extensively my harrowing, oftentimes, despairing experiences while living in that Romanian institution, the **"Hospital for Irrecoverable Children."**

Is that not a truly *hope-less* name?

## Prologue
### by Joan Bramsch

During the summer of 2001 I met Izidor Ruckel. I met him through another Romanian orphan, who had been adopted by a couple I knew, parent/subscribers of the ezine I've published for almost five years. The *Empowered Parenting Ezine* readers, most times, become my friends, as well. I value their determination to be good parents; they value my input, experience and advice.

Izidor had written a book, I was told, about his experiences as an abandoned child in Romania. Once I made the connection between him and his return trip with 20/20, I knew this was the reason why we were brought together. People the world over needed to read his true story and I could help him achieve that goal.

In reading his manuscript I discovered that he also needed to share with the reader more of his emotions through his senses, but he wasn't clear on how to do it so my skills as an investigative reporter became useful; I could ask Izidor the questions readers wanted answered. Then I blended his responses into the appropriate paragraphs.

Throughout the editing I made sure to keep the flavor of Izidor's work -- his *voice*, while ensuring the reader as much information as I could garner from his vast and deep memories of his horrendous experiences. To me, his internment seemed more like that of a child in a concentration camp during WW II. Truly, my heart filled with pain and tears blurred my vision as I read.

And yet, I have no pity for Izidor because, beyond any leaning toward that emotion, the young man will have none of it! Izidor Ruckel is a survivor of the highest order. He puts me in mind of a real life rendition of the character, Slip Mahoney, the pugnacious leader of the original, 1935, tough street gang in the movie series, **Dead End Kids**. Played by actor Leo Gorcey, Slip sometimes fractured his English, but nobody told him what to do, nobody was allowed to hurt members of his gang or their extended family, particularly those who were less able to fight for themselves and, though his powerful foes tried to beat him down, nobody could do it!

Unlike the actor, Izidor is Hollywood handsome! And although his courage and unswerving determination is like Leo's movie character, he is the real life model. He knows what his calling is in this life and he will find a way to make his Plan come true. And he will never, never, never, ever give up!

I think that's what attracted me to his cause in the first place; we share a tenacity to succeed. I consider it my honor to assist him.

Sincerely,

Joan Bramsch
http://www.EmpoweredParent.com

# Foreword

I am Izidor Ruckel and have recently celebrated my twenty-second birthday. For my first eleven years, I was one of the hidden orphans of Romania. Abandoned by my parents as a baby I was raised by the state in the *Hospital for Irrecoverable Children* – a secret place, unknown by the outside world, where children, from babies to the age of eighteen years, were hidden away because we were considered "rejects from the human race" by the state.

We were a mixture of every type of Special Needs child you might imagine – emotionally, mentally and physically, we were deemed unworthy of a normal existence – and so we were shut away from the public eye, condemned to a life that was both horrific and ugly. It was also dangerous.

There was never enough food or medical attention, nor were there enough caregivers to meet our varied needs and so, often, we took care of one another as best we could. Try though we might, in our childish, uneducated ways, it was never good enough, even for a modicum of "normal" life. But we knew no other, so it was normal for us.

I was blessed to escape that hell on earth and come to America, but there are many other of my friends who still live there. Some of them have now reached the age of eighteen years and have been transferred to the *Old Folks Home* to live among the elder special needs castoffs of the state. I have made a vow to rescue as many of them as I can. A large percentage of the profits from this book will assist me in making my dream come true.

This then, is my story.

**ROMANIA**

Some Romanian facts to give you an overview of the poorest country in the Eastern European block.

Population is 22.5 million.

The capital is Bucharest, where many of the nation's discarded children live beneath the streets, in the sewers of the city.

The language is Romanian and the literacy rate is a surprising 96.7%, particularly in comparison to the institutionalized children who have a virtual zero rate!

The monetary unit is the lieu; $1US = 33,300 leu.

Main exports are textiles and footwear, metal products, machinery and minerals.

The average annual income is $1,670, which is exacerbated by a 22% inflation rate.

And yet, the rate is slowing decreasing and the GDP of 4% is the highest among those poor nations.

Last, they have a tiny foreign debt compared to other nations -- only US$1.4 billion.

## Chapter One

*Romania* is a country in Eastern Europe. The country was part of the Roman Empire during ancient times, and its name means "land of the Romans." The countries on its borders are *Moldova, Ukraine, Hungary* and *Yugoslavia*.

Communists took over the Romanian government in the 1940's. At first, they ran the country according to the wishes of the Soviet Union, which was Europe's strongest communist nation. The Industrial Revolution changed Romania from an agricultural country to an industrial one, and the people were not prepared for this change.

The country became even more hopeless when *Nicolae Ceausescu* came into power in 1974 as the first President of Romania. A modern despot he led the Romanian Dark Age under Communism. Because Ceausescu and his communist party were in heavy debt, he decided to reduce the food costs, medicines and other basic necessities of the citizens, which drove Romania's people from a state of relative economic well-being to near starvation.

While Ceausescu and his wife (Elena) lived in high luxury, the rest of the country struggled to survive the poverty that was created long ago but had gotten worse through his rule. To make matters worse, Ceausescu believed there was strength in numbers so he wanted the Romanian population to be the largest population in the world, and he instituted terrible means to make it come true. He outlawed all birth control methods and decreed that every family have a minimum of five children.

This is how the Romanian population grew so quickly. Babies were conceived to families who were not able to take care of more children because they had so little money. It was a horrible dilemma for the parents, but they believed there was no choice; to save the older members of a family, the newborn members had to be sacrificed. Thus, began the terrible abandonment of babies to the state.

You may wonder why families didn't have the money to take care of their children? It was because the low monthly income in Romania was barely enough for one person, much less a family! People working in Romania, even today, can barely make $1,000 a year. In order to provide the basic needs of food and shelter for the children and the parents, the adults have to work two full-time jobs if they can find them, as well as, any part-time work they can find, most of the time, earning less than twenty-cents an hour in wages.

With this heavy burden and no choice as to family size, many parents were unable to keep their children at home with them. Everywhere you looked, you saw babies, babies, and more babies, all over Romania, being abandoned. Most children who were abandoned had disabilities of one form or another, ranging from physical diseases, mental retardation, emotional illnesses, physical handicaps, brain damage and problems controlling pent up anger and rage.

It's no wonder that many children were born with disabilities; the fathers and the mothers were malnourished to the point of starvation and the mothers-to-be had no prenatal care or special vitamins. Romanians of childbearing age were only expected to be baby machines for the glory of the state and of Ceausescu, but it didn't turn out that way and it was the children who paid the price! Often a child paid with his life.

The institutions that housed the Special Needs children were hidden from the world because, even though Romania's population was increasing as Ceausescu wished, many of the children were coming into this world with disabilities. He did not want the world to know that Romania had a great population of children with "unacceptable" disability problems so he hid them away and tried to forget them!

During this time, about eighty percent of the Romanian children were abandoned for life. **For life!** Where I grew up, in the *Hospital for Irrecoverable Children*, between 400 and 500 other children also lived in that ugly, ill-equipped "prison," where the once white walls were scarred and dirty and every floor was made of cold, rough concrete, stained from urine and feces, impossible to make clean again.

Among those hundreds and hundreds, there were very few children who ever received a visit from their parents. Where I grew up, and in other of the hidden institutions, many of the children died because of lack of care, the need for medication, the use of dirty needles for injections and because they never received the nurture, the love, a child needs to thrive. We were warehoused for life.

**Only those of us with the will to live, survived!**

Today Romania still has over 160,000 abandoned children living in the institutions. Although the free world has come to the children's aid, the scene continues to be tragic. It is even worse for the "normal" children who reach a certain age, like twelve or thirteen years (although they appear to be only eight- or nine-years old due to mal nourishment), and are forced to leave the state institutions to fend for themselves, with no education, no trade, no shelter. They usually end up begging in the streets, stealing, or selling their bodies for food, and then later, for drugs so they can forget what they are doing to survive.

These are the children, at least the ones who are still alive, who were interviewed originally in 1993 by reporters from the *ABC News 20/20* program. They lived in the sewers of the city, sharing the meager molding shelter of the underground with rodents, spiders and other germ-laden creatures. The scene has not changed, and has only grown worse because **now these children are giving birth to children in the sewers!**

Do you wonder why I feel I must help my Romanian brothers and sisters? *Camin Spital*, where I grew up, in the poor mountain village of *Sighetu Marmatiei*, was one of the hospitals hidden from the world for eleven terrible years of my life. At age thirteen years I too would have been told to leave, so there, but for the grace of God, go I! If you don't know about the 20/20 programs you can read the transcripts here:

http://www.johnupton.net/2020Transcript.htm

Because of the damage that Ceausescu had done to the country and to the people, it was time to fight back for what was taken away from the people. Homes, farms, and many other possessions were confiscated; so too were the people's self respect and basic freedoms.

For example, Ceausescu had construction companies build large, shoddy apartment complexes to house people whose property and farmland were taken. The plan was to displace 11,000,000 rural people from their home farms into 5-story urban structures. He did not give much thought to how he would feed the people without the home farms. I doubt he cared. On some of the land he built a palace. He also instituted a new "scientific" diet, which restricted food stuffs to the population, in order to have more product for export. For the first time in 27 years, bread was rationed.

When the people rose up to protest their treatment, the Romanian government finally did something about Ceausescu's crimes. He and his wife Elena tried to escape from justice in a helicopter fleeing Romania, but the military gave chase and they were eventually captured.

Inside a wooden schoolhouse, after being held captive for three days, Nicholae and Elena Ceausescu were condemned to death by a military tribunal whose authority they rejected. Their hasty and particularly gruesome execution fueled popular views

that they were silenced to conceal the misdeeds of others in the government. In Romania's capital Bucharest, on Christmas Day, 1989 they were shot dead by a firing squad for their crimes against the state and its people.

After Nicolae and Elena's death, the country began to improve slowly and a lot of changes were made for the better. Eventually, a new government was set up, and a new president was elected. Since that time, a president can only run for two four-year terms in office and is elected by the people, not by the government. And yet, Romania continues to be the poorest country in Europe and is a decade behind the economies of the surrounding countries.

Now, let us go back ten years, before Ceausescu was executed, and look at how our lives, the orphan's lives, were spent in the hospital in *Sighetu Marmatiei, Maramures, Romania*.

---

## Chapter Two

### The beginning of Izidor Bojani's Life

As far as I know, I was born in a small town in Northern Romania, *Sighetu Marmatiei*. Soon after I was born, my parents put me in the *Camin Spital Pentru Daficienti Coppi* (**Home Hospital for Irrecoverable Children**). They put me there because I was crippled. Later, doctors in America told me that I had probably contracted polio as a newborn and my lower limbs wasted away from lack of proper care and physical therapy. Once my parents abandoned me, they never returned to see how I was doing. Not once!

One of the first things I can remember at the hospital was the kindness of a lady who took care of me as if I were her own son. It was like a miracle and, surely, not what usually happened to the children there. The lady's name was Maria and she was one of the hospital's house nannies. She brought shampoo and clothes to me, and sometimes bits of food from her own home.

Not very many of the house nannies would do that for the children because they did not have loving hearts like Maria. It must have also been difficult to care even a little for just one of us when there were so many. Sometimes over 500 *special needs* children were jammed into that one building.

It seemed like many of the house nannies hated me because Maria favored me so much. She always tried to protect me from the other nannies and their cruel treatment. I often dreamed a dream… that she **was** my mother! But it was not meant to last.

A few years after I came to the hospital, there was a terrible accident. It all began one winter morning as all the children were being wakened out of bed at six o'clock. It was a bitter cold and snowy day, and children needed to take their baths. This was a daily ritual, no matter the weather, because many of the children, even the older ones, wet their beds every night. Even if a child did not wet the bed, oftentimes the child with whom he or she slept did wet the bed; thus, getting everything and every body soiled.

We were often forced to sleep together because there were not enough beds or cots to sleep singly. We would lie on the urine-saturated sheets, foot to head, head to foot, hoping we wouldn't get kicked as we tried to sleep. But in winter, when the frigid cold swept down through the mountain passes and we had no heat, sleeping together was welcomed, simply for sharing a bit of body warmth.

The hospital did not have a water heater for bath water so the house nannies heated the water by using an electrical coffee heater. In hindsight, it's amazing to me that they ever managed, even though a "bath" was more a dribble of water in the tub, rather than an opportunity to enjoy the luxury and warmth of deep clean water upon our skin.

One day, my surrogate mother Maria heated the water for baths on a different floor. The worn electrical wire must have been frayed and been exposed because there was a sudden flash of light, a loud popping sound, and Maria was electrocuted, dying quickly. At least that's the story I remember the other house nannies told me about how she died. That cold morning was the last time I ever saw Maria's smile or heard her cheerful voice. I will never forget that loving woman for all she did for me. Among the hospital workers, Maria was the kindest woman I had ever known. I will always carry her memory with me in my heart. I loved her and I believe that she loved me.

~~~~~~~~~~~~~~~~~~~~~~~~~~~~~

## Chapter Three

### This is how things went at the hospital, Monday through Friday.

The hospital is located in an ugly tall structure of gray concrete with barred windows and a flat roof. When I first arrived there, still a baby, the building rose from a great expanse of empty land. By the time I left ten years later, it was surrounded by dozens of other shoddy multistory buildings that housed displaced farm families.

Dormitories on each hospital floor were sectioned off, mostly according to age, with the babies on the first floor, the older girls on the second, the young to early teen boys and girls on the third, and the older boys on the fourth floor, but those of us who could, helped take care of the younger children. The other two floors were closed for lack of beds, and certainly not children.

When there wasn't total chaos, it was somewhat orderly. At least, you could identify the different types of employees by the color of their uniforms. For example, the house nannies in charge of cleaning the bedroom floors wore blue uniforms. They covered their hair with a triangular dark scarf tied in back. The house nannies, who worked with the children, wore green uniforms and white head scarves or nurse's caps. All the nurses and the cooks wore white uniforms. The nurses wore old-fashioned white, starched caps to show their authority over the other women employees, I think. The visiting doctor and the hospital's director wore long white lab coats over shirt and trousers.

Here is the schedule we followed. It never changed. *Ever!*

At 5:00 a.m., we were awakened from our beds. Those who had had an "accident" during the night and those who had not, were sent naked into the bathroom area. It made no difference if it was the dead of winter. We shivering naked children waited, staying out of the way for a very long time, sitting or standing on the rough pee-wet concrete floor while the house nannies changed the beds and cleaned the bedroom floors. And yet, the place always carried the stench of urine and excrement.

The soiled bedding was carried down to the laundry room at the back of the building on the first floor where there was only one washer and one dryer, old, noisy, barely running, but commercial size, to do the laundry for 500 babies and children! The laundry workers did not work with the children, but once in a while they did come up and visit us. When the house nannies were moved around, working on different floors, sometimes the workers from the laundry room were moved up to work with the children. These changes were always up to the director.

At seven o'clock, a new shift came on duty and finished the work the earlier shift had started. From 7:00 a.m. through three in the afternoon we had three house nannies working on each floor. That was only three nannies for a floor that housed between 100 and 150 *special needs* children.

Breakfast was served at 8:00 a.m. All the children on each floor came together to eat in two "eating" rooms where we sat on old wooden benches at long narrow tables. Two nannies went down to the kitchen to bring the breakfast up to us. The menu never varied: we always had bread soaked in milk. **That was all we had to eat at breakfast for nine years straight!** Perhaps ten years later, this is still all they get for breakfast.

The food was served with long dippers from big pots, blackened by age and flame, into dented metal bowls with chipped enamel on the outside and a spoon. Never, at any meal, were we served drinks – milk, tea, coffee, even water. If we wanted something to drink, we left the table and went to the bathroom to suck water directly from the sink faucet, but we only did that *after* we finished eating our food.

It didn't take us long to eat and after we were done, the house nannies washed the dishes in the bathroom sink, just as they did after every meal. I believe they just rinsed them off under the cold water without using any dish soap. There was probably none to be had. Those of us who survived our years in that hospital must have a formidable immune system, to have lived with all those germs!

After the dishes were finished, it was then that we were given our baths and dressed in clean clothes. Yes, your mental image is, no doubt, correct… we did eat breakfast, clothed only in our skin… and goose bumps! It's a wonder any of us lived. Actually, many of the children were never dressed because of a handicap or affliction.

Before the hidden children were discovered by the outside world I have no idea where the clothes we wore were found. I do know that, if there weren't enough clean clothes, I often had to wear girl's sweaters and slacks and, sometimes, girl's shoes. We boys felt lucky that we never had to wear dresses!

After getting dressed we were put into one of the clean rooms until lunchtime, with no games, no toys, no music. Just children, mostly screaming, crying, wailing children. Many of the mentally or emotionally challenged children either rocked back and forth or cried disconsolately while other children repeatedly hit themselves hard across the face. Sometimes they would stop for a few moments when we sang to them, but it didn't last for long.

If the children did not stop crying when they were told, the house nannies slapped them until they did stop crying. But when the children were slapped, they'd cried even more. They were hit many times before they finally overcame the pain and stopped themselves from crying out. Obviously, the house nannies were not always patient with the children.

Sometimes they would get so frustrated by the constant crying and screaming that they'd give up altogether and drug the children to keep them quiet. When the medications were given to the children, they would sleep for three or more hours. The house nannies used drugs often for this purpose.

While the drugged children were quiet or sleeping, the house nannies just sat around chatting to each other. By the time the children woke up, it was lunchtime. For lunch we had noodle and water soup, beans, or other side dishes like cornmeal mush, again served in the old, paint chipped, dented metal bowls. Many of the children could not learn to use their spoons so they slurped their meal directly from their bowls.

After we children were done eating our noon meal, we were put into another cleaned room to, again cry, rock, scream, hit or entertain ourselves. There was not a toy, a ball, a piece of string, nothing with which we could play. Most of the time, the children did the same old thing; rock back and forth, sleep or hurt themselves. If they continued hurting themselves, the house nannies either gave the children more medication or put them into straight jackets. To my knowledge, doctors were never consulted about this behavior; the nannies just "handled" it. But I suppose the doctors gave the nannies the drugs in the first place.

At 3:00 p.m., a new shift came on duty. We usually had two house nannies working on each floor for the afternoon shift, a ratio of one nanny per 75 to 80 children. Most of the time, children were much quieter in the afternoon. I think they may have still been drugged from the morning doses. Often the house nannies left their posts and their charges, and went on other floors to visit with the other employees. I was often put in charge of my peers when they left; a little child expected to take care of an army of other little children in any way I found feasible. I often mimicked the house nannies' methods.

Every night for supper, we had macaroni with red jelly smeared over it, rice and milk mixed together, and spinach or something else green (not counting the mold!). I suppose one could deduce that we got a balanced diet – carbohydrates, sugar, a bit of protein, calcium and minerals. I can tell you this: it tasted bad and for the rest of my life I hope I never have to eat such nasty food again.

After dinner children were given their baths again before going to bed. The second bath was necessary because so many of the children were either not toilet-trained or incontinent for emotional or physical reasons. There were no diapers, not cloth ones, and certainly not disposable ones. Instead, if the babies or incontinent children wore anything at all, it was a folded piece of old sheet or a ragged towel fastened between their legs. Most of the time, if nude, the child simply stood there and his pee would arch across the floor, or run down her legs, making a warm puddle for her bare feet. If dressed, the clothing simply got more wet and smelly.

Although there were several toilets on each floor, only the one in the eating rooms was ever used. I do not know the reason why this was true. Instead, the children were given small bowls to sit upon. No toilet paper, no clean up when the containers tipped over and spilled, just small bowls into which the children relieved themselves… sometimes. If they were physically unable to contain themselves or too mentally or emotionally impaired to remember, then the bowls were useless; the elimination happened where they stood or sat or crawled or rolled.

Usually after the children ate their dinner, they were given drugs again before being paired into their rusty, paint chipped beds. At 9:00 p.m., a new shift came on duty. One house nanny was scheduled to work on each floor during night shifts – that's **one nanny for every one-hundred fifty children.**

She would go around all the rooms to make sure all the children were asleep or at least in bed. If the children were quiet in bed or asleep, the house nanny would go to sleep, too. This was against the rules; house nannies were supposed to stay awake all through the night. If the director had been there, they would have been awake, all right! At 5:00 a.m. it started all over again when we were wakened and told to get out of our urine-soaked beds.

That's how things went at the hospital for the ten years I lived there. Some of us sensed that it was not right treatment, but there was nothing we could do to change it.

# Chapter Four

## New Workers

There were many house nannies who were either fired or retired, but there were always new house nannies to replace the ones who left. The economy was bad and jobs were hard to find. During that time, there was also a new director who replaced our old one.

The new director's name was Viorel. Viorel was six feet tall, skinny, with black short hair and dark skin. Although he didn't wear a uniform, in a way, he did. Every day he wore the same dark gray trousers, white shirt and no tie, with a light gray cardigan sweater and his long white doctor's coat. When he left at night, he'd exchange the white coat for his gray suit jacket. His black dress shoes showed long wear, but were never dusty or scuffed.

He was a fair man, but he did have two bad habits. Every time he came on a floor to see us, he always had a lit cigarette in his hand. He carried the pack in the top pocket of his white coat. Sometimes, when he was short on money he bought what are called "rollies;" that is, someone rolled the tobacco in papers and charged less for them than the packs cost. He also had a drinking problem. Looking back as an adult I can understand how nervous he must have felt and also how hopeless at times. His was a thankless job.

Over the years, there were at least thirty new house nannies who were hired to work at our hospital. Marika, one of the workers, told me that the daughter of Maria, my beloved nanny who was electrocuted, was working here at the Camin Spital. I did not believe her until she called Rodica, and had her tell me herself. I liked Rodica simply because she was Maria's daughter and I hoped we would get along like her mother and I did. It wasn't the same, but still, she was nice to me.

Three of the new house nannies were put on the floor where I lived to work with us. Most of the new workers were actually much nicer to us than the other house nannies who had been working at the hospital for a longer period of time. I think it was because they still had some energy. Also, there were more nannies to care for the children so the workload was less.

Unfortunately, among the new house nannies, there was one who loved to abuse children. Her name was Felicia, which, ironically, means "happy." The woman only seemed to enjoy herself when she was beating children! At times, she was so out of control that other house nannies had to tell her that she needed to leave the kids alone.

Some of us tried hitting Felicia back, but no matter how hard we hit her, she always hit us back harder with all her strength. It was a terrible experience, especially for the children who couldn't help their behavior. At night I would plan revenge, but I knew I couldn't really do anything about the woman because I had no power.

Sometimes Director Viorel came up to see how we were doing. He knew that some things were not right, and he'd ask us if anyone ever hit us? We never told him anything because we were all scared of Felicia, and also of a second nanny, who was almost as bad, named Anna. If we even said one of their names, we knew they'd punish us severely. There were many times when I just wanted to tell Viorel who was beating us, but I was too scared, especially of Anna.

### Onisa and Anna

One afternoon, Onisa and Anna were scheduled to work on the floor where I lived. That shift, Onisa was in charge of all the children. She asked me to keep the kids quiet and to clean the floors. I did as I was told and from the heart.

Onisa was never mean to me as long as I can remember. That is why I did things for her with a willing heart. She was a young lady, a bit chubby, with long black hair and round rosy cheeks. She loved to sing and she often taught us some of her music. My favorite song that she'd sing was *"When I was home, I loved my daughter."* She didn't work long at our hospital. I don't think she liked seeing us being beaten, but she was good to me while she was there.

Anna had worked at the hospital since 1973, almost fifteen years. She had short black hair, but always dyed it henna red. Her eyes were small and beady with drawn on black brows. Her sallow skin sagged with age and attitude: she never smiled. The following afternoon, she and Onisa were again scheduled on the same shift, but this time Anna was in charge of all the kids.

"Izidor, make sure all the kids are quiet and are not running around," Anna told me.

Doing jobs for Anna was not always a work from the heart. That afternoon, Anna exploded when she saw many of the children, naked, and crying. The rough cement floors were covered in urine, from children peeing on the floor or in their clothes. Children were sliding their butts in the urine and splashing their hands into puddles of pee.

"Izidor," she scolded, "why are the kids crying and why does it smell so bad in the room?"

I kept trying to clean up the mess. It was hard to push around the mop when I could hardly stand up because of my weak legs. Out in the hallway, when Anna got tired of hearing the kids crying and yelling, she lost control and came back into the room with a thick oak broomstick, heading for me. Screaming hysterically, she beat me for not taking care of the kids. She was so angry I thought she would kill me.

Finally, she dressed the children and cleaned up the urine from the floor. Afterwards, she again told me to keep them quiet and I tried my best, but I was just a child myself, a child who could barely walk. When she told me to help her put the kids to bed, as usual, she was not satisfied with my work. For punishment, she tried to slap me – I was not working fast enough to suit her, but before she could get her hands on me, Onisa stopped her.

Still, she was not quick enough to keep me from cowering. Every time one of the house nannies raised their hand to me, I'd instantly cover my head with my hands to protect myself from being hit on the head. Onisa took me into a different room and told me that one of these days she would take me home with her. I felt a lot better when she told me that.

Onisa had to leave work early that night, around 8:00. Anna put me in bed first, and I watched her bathe the children and put them to bed. She kept yelling at all the kids, so Chobbie, my chubby friend with the black hair that always fell forward into his eyes, and I decided to imitate everything that she said. Unfortunately for us, she eventually heard our echo of her words.

Silently, like Death, she walked into another room and returned with the thick oak broomstick. Silently, she strode toward my bed and I began to truly fear for my life. Completely out of control again, she angrily tore off my tattered blanket, raised the broomstick over her head and beat me almost senseless. It hurt me so bad I thought she had broken many of my bones, surely a rib or two. After she was done with my beating, she turned and started beating Chobbie until she had no more strength left to wield her weapon. Then she left, as silently as she had come... like Death!

Chobbie was in as bad a condition as I was because, he too, couldn't run away from Anna. Chobbie was about my age, about eight at the time, and he was never able to walk on his feet. Because he never had a wheelchair, he had to instead crawl around on his knees. His hands were crippled, too, and bent inward so he had to use his knuckles for hand balance, much like a great ape, as he moved about on his knees.

That night, I could barely move my body. That's how much it hurt after being beaten by Madwoman Anna, but I think that Chobbie and I both learned our lesson that night. There was no room for humor in the Home of the Irrecoverable Children.

At times the other house nannies were frightened by Anna, as well. Everything had to be cleaned up and organized before Anna came on duty or else! The woman was a tyrant, and she took sadistic pleasure in the beatings she gave to us children.

A few weeks after Anna beat Chobbie and me, Onisa finally asked me if I wanted to go home with her. I was so excited when she asked me. If I could escape, even for a few hours, I would be grateful. To tell you the truth, I didn't think she would keep her word, but Onisa was not like the other house nannies who often lied to the children.

It was on a winter afternoon right after she got off work that she took me home with her. I was dressed in really nice clothes that were also very warm because it was cold and snowing outside. **This was the first time since I was brought here as a baby that I had ever been out of the hospital building because we were kept hidden from the world.** I had never felt grass beneath my feet nor, like now, felt the snow crunching beneath my shoes. I shall never forget it. Never!

As we walked to her home, I looked around me to see what the city looked like, since it was my first time ever going out in the world. I wanted to remember it all, to tell my friends at the hospital. I had no idea when, or if, it would ever happen again.

When I stepped into Onisa's apartment, I could not believe how beautiful it was; the walls were covered with dark rugs and there was a picture of the *Last Supper* on one of them. The carpets on the floor were red. The bathroom was really small and so was the kitchen, but I didn't care whether the house was big or small. I was out of the hospital and I loved being in a home.

Shortly after we got to the apartment, there was a knock at the door. When Onisa went to see who was there, she found some neighbor kids who asked if I wanted to come outside to play with them. I went, gladly. When I went outside, the kids asked me a lot of questions about me living in a hospital. I answered, gladly, too.

I had so much fun being at Onisa's house that towards 5:00 in the evening I had forgotten all about living in the hospital. I never wanted to go back. Ambulating around for me was really hard because of the disability I had, but back then, no one seemed to know how my disability came about.

That evening, Onisa's three kids came home from school. She told me they were now on vacation for the Christmas holiday. She had a daughter and two sons, Maria, Daniel and Ioan. Later, we all went to a place called a cemetery to visit the grave of one of Onisa's friends who had recently passed away. When we arrived at the cemetery, I was a bit scared because of all the holes that were dug in the ground. I feared I might fall in!

"Izidor, do you remember Evascu?" Onisa asked me.

"I remember Evascu. What about him?" I replied.
"This is where he was buried when he died."

When she told me that, I was even more scared, knowing that this was where people go after they die. The whole cemetery was full of praying people and flickering flames. Everywhere you looked, lit candles marked new graves or stood upon stones, revealing halos of light as the sky darkened. It was frightening; it was beautiful.

After some prayers, which sounded somewhat to me like a droning motor, we left the cemetery and went to the home of one of Onisa's friends. There, we ate dinner. And what a dinner it was! We feasted upon the traditional cabbage roll, offered especially at party or holiday celebrations, potato soup with thick noodles, sweet yellow sponge cake with cream filling, and tart lemonade poured from a bottle purchased, ready made, from a grocery store.

While Onisa and her friends visited, a small boy and I played on the floor with his cars and trains. He made "bruuum, bruuum" sounds as he raced the car I used. Boys in Romania, just as boys everywhere it seems, love to play with cars, trucks and trains. I could only imagine how wonderful it must be to have toys of one's own.

Around ten that night, we went back to Onisa's home and I went to sleep, smiling. In the morning when I woke up, Onisa was dressed as if she was going to work.

"Izidor, do you want to go to work with me," she asked, "or do you want to stay here with Daniel and Ioan?"

"I want to go to work with you," I replied.

I got dressed as fast as I could and we headed out the door to Onisa's work. When we were near her work, I realized that her work was at the hospital, **my hospital**, and I began to cry because I was being put back into the hospital. Only a child's mind would think this way: It had never occurred to me that her work was actually at the hospital until we were at the gate again.

I was heartbroken to have to go back into the hospital. I loved being at Onisa's house. It was one of the best things that happened to me in my whole life. That whole day, I cried and cried until the other house nannies were so tired of it that they told Onisa that she was stupid for taking me home with her, but she didn't care what they thought.

"Izidor, I need you to stop crying or I will not be allowed to take you home with me again."

I stopped crying instantly when she told me that. Being at Onisa's house, I felt like I was her son because she treated me so well and cared for me more than the rest of the house nannies did. She was the next Maria Petreus to take care of me and I prayed she would stay well and never leave me.

~~~~~~~~~~~~~~~~~~~~~~~~~~~~~~~

## Chapter Five

### Marian

Marian was at least eight years old when he was put in the *Camin Spital Pentru Deficienti Coppi*. When he first came to the hospital, he was chubby, hyperactive and loved to play. I don't know what Marian's disability was, because he walked normally and didn't seem to be disabled emotionally or mentally. I wonder if he was brought to this particular hospital because it was, perhaps, the closest institution to where his family lived? In his case, this would have been very important.

Why, you may ask? It was because Marian also had something that most children at the home only dreamed of having, parents who would visit often to see how he was doing. For most of us, that dream would never happen in our lifetimes. But for Marian, his father came to see him every Saturday afternoon.

Within a year or two, with no sunshine and no fresh air and a less than adequate diet, Marian became ill. He was put in bed until he could recover but, the thing is, he never did recover from his illness. Eventually, he lost his ability to walk on his own two feet. Weeks, months, and years went by and slowly Marian stopped eating his meals.

One afternoon, the house nannies were shorthanded. They asked me to help them feed all the children who were in bed. While I was in Marian's room, I decided to see if he would eat anything for me. Sure enough, he did. I went to tell a house nanny that he ate some of his cornmeal mush. She came back into the bedroom to see if he would eat for her. Again, Marian spit the food out of his mouth, but when I took over feeding him, he ate a few more spoonsful. I gave a shout, I was so happy, but poor Marian only wore a weak smile.

"From now on, Izidor will feed Marian and take care of him," Marika ordered.

She told his father that Marian was only eating for me and I was taking care of him. His father asked her to bring me downstairs to meet me in person. His father thanked me for taking care of his son. After I met his father, during the weeks that followed, I always went to the window to watch them as they talked outside like a father and son should.

On a Saturday afternoon in September, a rainy chill day with a bleak overcast sky, Marian's father came for his weekly visit, but no one knew this would be the last visit ever that his father would make to see his son. I don't know the reason, but Marian's father was not allowed to go upstairs to see his own son. Instead, two house nannies wrapped the boy in a warm blanket and took him to his father outside. After they took him downstairs, I went as usual to the window to watch. Sitting on a bench, the father embraced his son and began rocking him back and forth. It was sad for me to watch. Even from the fourth floor window I could see the grief and pain upon the man's features. He was sad, too.

Over the years, Marian had lost a tremendous amount of weight. You could almost see his bones through his skin; that's how sick he had become. I think his father sensed the seriousness of his son's illness. What I could not understand is why he did not take him out of the hospital to have him treated. Was he sick with an incurable disease? Would no doctor treat the boy because the father had no money? I did not know the answer; no one would tell me the truth. The situation will never be explained. It will remain a mystery for the rest of my life.

That day as Marian and his father spent time together, the boy passed away in his father's arms. Although he was dead, his

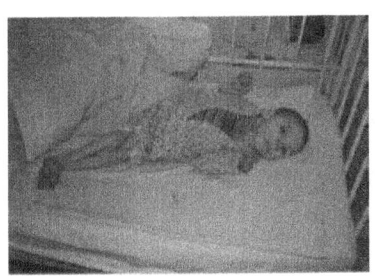

father continued to rock his son back and forth. He looked up towards the gray weeping sky and I could hear his cries and moans and see tears drip from his cheeks. He was heartbroken to lose his beloved son.

Sometime later, he carried Marian back upstairs and lay him on his bed. He kissed his son's forehead and left the room, crying. I wanted to call out to the father, to tell him I was sorry, to tell him that I would be his son so he could still come to visit each Saturday. Something in my heart stopped me.

Shortly after the man left the building, Marian's body was undressed, completely naked on his bed, covered only with a sheet. His body remained there for two or three hours before people from the morgue came. We all saw it. Frightening ourselves, we sat huddled together on the floor in the corner, peering at the bed sheet, watching closely, then swore that Marian's body breathed.

Marian may have died a painful and slow death, but at the time I looked at it this way: He was in Heaven with God, the One who created him in the first place. Marian no longer had to worry about being abused or to suffer any more of the pain that he had endured while he was alive. I still believe that is true.

### Duma

I'll tell you another story about a different boy who went through similar things that Marian experienced. His name was

Duma. He was put in the hospital at the same age as Marian, about eight years. He was hyperactive, loved to play around, and was also chubby. I do not know, to this day, what disabilities Marian or Duma suffered, but as for Duma, like me, his parents abandoned him for life. This is how Duma suffered differently from Marian. I think, being alone, made the suffering that much harder, too.

It all began on a summer evening, when all the children were being fed dinner. Duma did not want to eat his dinner that night. The house nannies tried forcing food into his mouth, but Duma spit the food right back out. They finally gave up and let him go to bed without eating his dinner. Duma was already as sick as Marian had been. He stopped eating and lost a tremendous amount of weight, as well.

At 9:00 p.m., a new shift came on duty. The house nanny who was scheduled to work on my floor was Anna. For some reason, I could not sleep that night, but I lay in bed, pretending to be asleep. I was afraid of Anna because she was so cruel to us.

That night, when Anna was asleep, I heard a noise that came from the hallway. I did not know who had gotten out of bed, but I saw Anna wake up and go investigate. When she got to the hallway, she caught a little boy, Duma, creeping along the wall. I turned on my side and saw Anna grab him by his shirt and drag him back to his bed. She picked him up and threw him in his bed. The boy began to cry.

"Stop crying, bad boy," she hissed. "Shut up or you'll wake the others."

But Duma could not stop crying. Anna got so upset that she hit him with her big bare hands. Her hands were hard as rock. Quite often she had used her hands to beat me so you can believe me when I say that it hurt almost as bad as being hit with the broomstick. The more she hit Duma, the more I began to tremble beneath my covers, but I did not stop watching from the peephole tear in the blanket.

The more she hit Duma with her hard bare hands, the more Duma cried. It seemed that the more Duma cried, the harder she hit him. Anna had finally had enough and lost complete control. She took off both her shoes and, with all the strength she had, she hit him with the heels.

Finally, Anna's beating stopped Duma's crying. He lay still in his bed. Then she turned and strode toward my cot and I thought I would die from fear. Was she going to beat me now? When she tore back my covers I cringed, waiting, but instead she shook me by the shoulder.

"Wake up," she whispered harshly. "You… Izidor, wake up."

I acted as if I were just waking from a deep sleep.

"Get up and watch the kids who are awake now," she ordered. "I have to rest."

I did as she ordered, but when she fell back to sleep, I sneaked into a different room and climbed into bed with another kid. I was too scared to go back to my own bed, which would be cold and wet by now anyway.

In the morning when I woke up, I swept and mopped all the bedroom floors. It was a favor that I was doing for another house nanny. When I got to Duma's room he was awake, but he lay very still. His shirt was ripped to pieces on the floor and no blanket covered him, but his body was covered with something terrible; all that was visible on him were welts and bruises. Anna's handiwork!

I promised I would come back for a visit, then hurried to finish my work by 8:00 a.m. and breakfast time. A house nanny went to feed Duma and all the other kids who were in bed. But for Duma, it was too late for breakfast because he was already dead.

Did anyone ever bother to ask, "Where did all those bruises come from?" No! Not one complaint! The staff looked the other way and just let the world believe that he had died like all the other children have died at the home throughout the years -- from illness.

Did I ever tell anyone that I knew how Duma really died? No, I never told anyone because I was scared for my life and they probably would not have believed me even if I had told. I was just a little kid, but this I know: Duma was killed, beaten to death by Anna. I kept my secret all these years. You are the first to hear it.

It's been terrible not to share it. Sometimes I feel ashamed and guilty for not saving my friend. Other times I still feel frightened and helpless. I don't know which feelings are the hardest to bear. I hope my friend up in Heaven has forgiven me. I still have not been able to forgive myself.

I'll tell you this, too: both Duma and Marian died at young ages and in awful ways. Looking back, I wonder if they got ill from getting shots with the dirty needles? People with AIDS look exactly like Duma and Marian did before they died. I wonder, too, if their parents had raised those two kids at home, would they still be alive today? I believe they would have lived and they would have been around my age. Their deaths were a terrible undeserved loss. Who knows what contribution they might have made to the world?

~~~~~~~~~~~~~~~~~~~~~~~~~~~~~~

## Chapter Six

### Disease Outbreak

You know, reader, it's hard for me to remember to call the place where I grew up a hospital, but that is what it was supposed to be, simply because the children who lived there were all special needs of one sort or another. Most of us -- the ones who could think and speak -- call it The Home. Wishful thinking!

When a child became ill at the hospital, s/he was usually given medications to help recover. At times, we were given shots, rather than pills but, whether we had a shot or a pill, our lives were always in danger, rather than being protected.

Needles were not sterilized when they were used on children, time after time. Now that I am grown, I believe that was one of the reasons why many of my friends died at the home. Even the pills had something wrong with them. The pills made us nauseated and caused vomiting. We couldn't even eat our meals without vomiting.

When the nurses gave us the shots, they were very rough with us, like they were punishing us for being sick. It was as if we caused them trouble, on purpose! Some of the nurses would take the needle off the syringe and poke us three times. On the third poke, they'd slam the needle into our skin and connect the syringe with the needle while it was already stuck in our flesh.

The way most of the nurses poked us, we couldn't stand still and ultimately we often ended up breaking the needle while they gave us the shot. At times, the needles broke in half. Sometimes it got swallowed up in the muscle and disappear. When that happened we would get hit so hard and slammed against the wall to wait while the nurse got another dirty needle to stick into us.

I was often given the pills as a form of punishment when I wasn't on my best behavior but, when the pills were given to me, they made me so sick I thought I would die. If I ate something, I vomited the food. There were times when I felt certain I would die and not see another day go by. Somehow I always ended up surviving through this mad sickness. It was as if God was watching over me and protecting me.

Most of the other kids were not so lucky. I believe that one of the main reasons children were getting sick and dying was because of the medications given to them. These drugs were not medications to help children recover from their illness but, rather, to shut them up. I do not believe that anyone ever noticed or cared that the medications were the reason why so many children were losing their lives.

Perhaps we children were guinea pigs for testing medicines or, perhaps, some of the nannies were insane and overdosed us, trying to kill us. I don't know the answer. It's another mystery.

It was not only the drugs that made the children ill. It was also the food that was served. Milk was spoiled; rice, buggy; greens, rotten; fats and oils, rancid. The food we were expected to eat was so nasty that no person could really enjoy eating it. But for us kids, it was either that or nothing.

Would you enjoy eating macaroni and red jelly almost every night, and milk and bread every morning? If the children did not like their meals, they would starve themselves. In most cases, they would end up losing a tremendous amount of weight and slowly turn into a dead-looking living being. Like a zombie! But, what the heck... these children didn't have a future, right? They were the rejects of Romania. That's why they were hidden away in the hospital!

Who did these children really belong to? According to the Romanian president, Nicolae Ceausescu, these children belonged to the Romanian Government's institutions. Even today, children living in any Romanian orphanage or hospital are the ones who end up paying the price. Not the parents or anyone else. Only the children end up suffering for someone else's mistake.

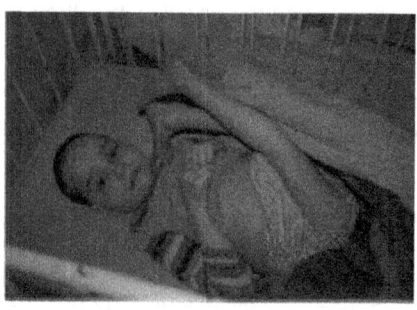

God did not give us life to waste it; rather, He gave us life in order to use it by helping another life that we bring into this world. Raise your children with love, respect and care with all your heart for what you have. Don't take things for granted or misuse them. Treat others, as you would want them to treat you in return. **That's all any of the orphans ever wanted -- to be loved.**

One evening, cruel Anna was scheduled to work on the fourth floor. That night, I had to help her with the younger children. My job was to bathe and dress them for bed. I had one boy who would not take his bath and I got so frustrated with the kid that I grabbed his hand and tried pulling him into the tub, but with my crippled legs, I ended up falling.

I grabbed the boy by his leg so he couldn't run out of the bathroom. The boy fell on the cement floor and broke open his head. When I got up, I saw blood going everywhere. I never meant for the boy to get hurt, but when I saw all that blood, I got scared. I knew I couldn't tell Anna the truth because she would probably beat me to death.

I quickly came up with a plan, praying it would work, when I saw a teenage boy walking by, in the hallway. "Come here," I shouted. "Help me with this boy."

He saw blood, took one look at me, and knew I was going to set him up.

"You broke his head open," I yelled. "Anna, come see what happened."

When Anna walked in, I was more scared then I thought I could ever be. Anytime I got scared of someone or scared something was going to happen to me, my face turned red. That's what happened when Anna came in; my face turned red. Anna looked at both of us and knew who had really caused the boy's injury.

"Izidor, you did it." That's all she said to me at that moment, because first she had to get the boy to the medical hospital, right across the street from our hospital.

After the boy was rushed to the hospital, Anna took me to a different floor, the one that housed the older children. There, she left me with kids, who were between the ages of fifteen and eighteen years old, while she went to speak with Maria.

"I think we're going to get a job to do on this little guy," said one boy who appeared to be the leader of the group. He gazed down at me and I began to tremble. "You must of done something real bad to get brought up here to us."

After awhile, Anna came back and told all the kids to jump me and beat me up. At that time, I must have been about seven years old. There wasn't anything I could do to defend myself. While Anna watched, I was beaten by kids twice my age and size. Then she calmly walked me back to my floor, waited while I washed the blood from my nose and cleaned the cuts on my face, then put me to bed. For the rest of the night, I lay awake, frightened for my life, waiting for her return.

In the morning, I woke up and other house nannies asked me what had happened to me. I was all bruised up from being beaten. I told them Anna beat me. Once I said Anna's name, it ended the discussion; nobody crossed Anna about anything. The boy who fell in the bathroom had only a few stitches on his forehead and soon returned to the home as if nothing had happened. **But I remember that beating to this day!**

~~~~~~~~~~~~~~~~~~~~~~~~~~~~~~~

## Chapter Seven

### Hidden from the world

Camin Spital was one of the hospitals hidden from the world for the first nine years of my life. Why would someone hide these orphanages and hospitals? The Romanian president, Nicolae Ceausescu, considered us a shame and disgrace to the country because of our disabilities.

Here are some of the disabilities of the children at the hospital; they ranged from physical diseases like AIDS and tuberculosis, to mental retardation, emotional illnesses, physical handicaps and brain damage. There were also perfectly fine children who had epilepsy, a condition easily treated with the correct drugs, and bright children who were blind. Like me, their condition had nothing to do with their ability to function in the outside world, and yet, we were hidden because we were different from what was considered the norm.

All were jammed together into the same space, 500 children, from age three years to eighteen years, in an ill-equipped building that should have barely accommodated half that number. There was no separation except by age, and even that rule didn't always hold because we children had to take care of each other.

When a child was born and abandoned at birth s/he was placed in the *Longan De Copii* (Rocking the children) hospital. Once they turned three years old, they were transferred to another orphanage or hospital, but before the child could be transferred, doctors checked to see if s/he was disabled or not. If the child was disabled, then s/he would be placed in a "hidden" orphanage or hospital with less fortunate children and no opportunities for a future.

However, if the child did not have a disability, then s/he was placed into a different kind of orphanage. Those children sometimes went to school and were allowed to go out in public and participate in outside activities. Most of the better orphanages were in Bucharest and the disabled institutions were located in the less accessible mountainous north, where the "misfits" were more easily hidden, but *none* of the institutions were good.

Most children at the hospital had never been outside the hospital building. They had been hidden in the building for years. Some kids were fifteen to eighteen years old and had never been outside in their lives! I had the opportunity to go outside of the hospital only when I went home with Onisa a few times. Is it any wonder that many of us were sickly? No sunshine, no exercise, no fresh air.

Back in the early 1980s, when Romania's President Ceausescu was known as one of the worst Communist dictators in the world, women who could not afford to take care of their children abandoned them. The question is, what happened to the unwanted children when all the orphanages and hospitals were filled to overflowing?

**Children were put out on the streets and some newborns were dumped into trash cans.**

After Elena and Nicolae Ceausescu were executed for their crimes in December, 1989, the world began finding out about the hidden orphanages and hospitals. Charitable groups and other national governments rushed to help the country. The world also began adopting children from orphanages and hospitals, who needed a home and a family.

## Chapter Eight

### First visit from Germany

One morning, Director Viorel received a telephone call from Germany. The Germans told him they were coming to the hospital to see the children. After he got off the phone, he ordered every house nanny on duty to clean the building, top to bottom, inside and out. Some of us children had to help with the cleanup, too. It took a whole day to do a halfway decent job of it. The Germans would be the first people to visit our hospital after the execution of Ceausescu. A week later, the Germans arrived and saw the conditions in which we lived.

Most of the children became hysterical when they first saw the Germans. They cried because they had never before seen anyone with a long beard, and that terrified them. For the most part, all the Germans did was count how many children lived on each floor. After they were done counting, they went outside. I looked out the window to see them drive away in two vans.

Shortly after they left, Marika asked me to put some shoes on the window so they could dry in the sun. I looked out and saw that they had returned with four large trucks filled with donations for us. The gifts and supplies were not given directly to the children but, rather, put into a storage unit until they were sorted out. It took almost the whole day to unload the trucks. Most of us children watched from the windows since we were not allowed to go outside.

All the donations remained in storage for about a week. Then the director allowed each of the house nannies to take home a sack filled with bedding and clothes. That was the last we saw of those first donations. We children never received one thing! The rest was either sold on the Black Market or stolen. Even the medications were sold on the streets for high prices, rather than being used for what they were intended, to save the lives of children!

After the first visit from the Germans, word seemed to spread and organizations from around the world began donating medical supplies, clothing, bedding, toys and blankets for the children in orphanages and hospitals all over Romania. Sometimes the orphan children actually got some of the supplies! Donations, including Bibles, were even given to homeless children, who lived in the sewers and canals of the capital, and adults on the streets.

One of the items that helped the children immensely, was disposable needles on the syringes. They saved lives if used properly. After a nurse used a disposable syringe, she threw it into a trash can. I sometimes took them out of the trash cans and injected children with urine and water mixed together because the color was similar to one of the tonics we were given. I had done this quite a few times on many children and, at age eight years, I had absolutely no idea what harm I might have done to them.

The last time I injected anyone with urine and water was one morning, right after the children were wakened. Marika asked me to make sure none of the kids were running around or screaming. While she roused the children, one by one, I went to the trash can and retrieved a syringe. Taking it apart I peed a dribble into the syringe and mixed it with water until it compared in color to one of the medications. Now I could play doctor! I walked up to a kid and injected him. I'd done it so often that I could inject him as good as the nurses did, fast and quick.

This time something went wrong and the boy screamed and began to cry. Marika came back into the room to see why the boy was screaming. When she saw the boy's swollen, bruised leg she knew it was either caused by a beating... or by being injected with urine and water by a child who didn't realize he was being wicked!

Marika looked around to see who had hurt the child, and I quickly threw the syringe under the table, but I was too late. She saw what I had done, but because she was so busy trying to get all of her work done before the 7:00.a.m. shift came on duty, she didn't punish me, although she did tell the other house nannies what I had done. I expected to be beaten and I still cannot understand why none of them did anything to me for injecting the kid. On my own, I decided it wasn't a nice thing to do so I stopped.

Another time I found a new matchbook. I took the matches into the trash room and began lighting paper. As I was lighting my first match, Cardos came into the room to see what I was doing. As I lit my second match to the paper, the flame flared up and I accidentally burned Cardos' left eye. For the first few days his eye looked normal, but about a week later his left eye turned pink and looked infected, and I noticed it right away.

"Cardos, if the house nannies ask you who did this to you, what are you going to tell them?" I asked.

"Tibi did this to me, is what I'll tell them."

"Good," I said. "Do not tell them that I did that to you."

If something happened to one of the children at the hospital, I was always the one to be blamed for the accidents. Most of the time, I was the one that should have been blamed. When I was blamed for Cardos' pink eye I expected to be beaten, but the house nannies never did anything to me. I think they must have been too tired to chase after me, or else they just didn't care.

~~~~~~~~~~~~~~~~~~~~~~~~~~~

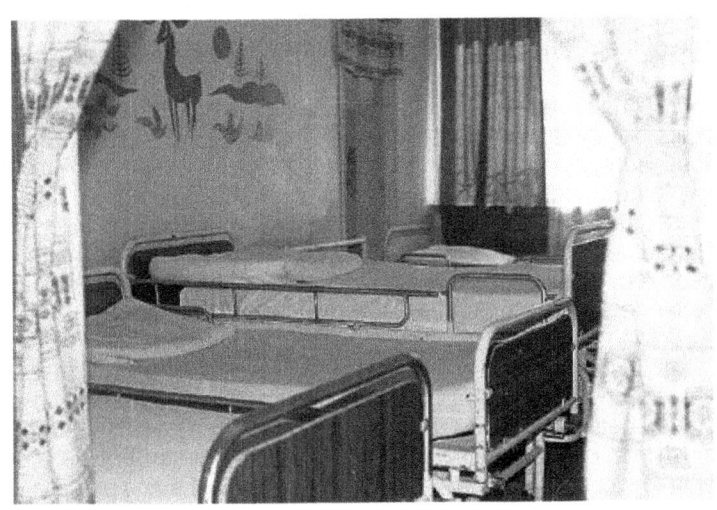

## Chapter Nine

### Changing Lives

At the hospital there were two floors that had been closed for years, primarily because we did not have enough beds for everyone. Every child had to share a bed with another. Now, since relief agencies donated beds, the director planned to reopen those floors, along with other changes around the hospital, including hiring new house nannies. It took about six months to complete the refurbishing.

Many of the walls were decorated with stenciled animal designs; before that, all the soiled walls were a drab dull white. New beds replaced the cot beds, which looked like prison beds, rusty metal with ugly chipped paint. Plastic greenery nailed on walls, made the rooms appear more pleasant. Carpets now covered the center of the hallways so children sat there, instead of on cold cement. Half a year later, it seemed as if a new orphanage had been built.

The new floors were designated for kids who could learn and walk on their own feet. It broke the hearts of some children left behind with the same mean house nannies. Thank God, I was not one of them, and I soon moved onto the new third floor.

I had lived on the fourth floor since I was not quite three years old and abandoned, but now I was glad to go to the third floor. Here, our lives began to slowly change for the better. Almost all the new house nannies worked on the third floor with us. They treated us much better. We began getting better food, and we started getting some education, but only on the two floors that had been reopened. I did not realize it then, but now I know we got better care because the world was watching!

Instead of having milk and bread every day for breakfast, we got tea, and sometimes hot chocolate with crackers. For lunch we started getting *Sarmale* (cabbage roll), *mamaliga cu brinza* (corm mush with cheese), *si mai bine supa* (better soups). Sarmale is one of the favorite foods served at holiday celebrations and parties.

Another big change after the move: children were taken outdoors for the first time in their lives, to play and breathe the fresh air. Weeks later, we actually went off the hospital grounds. We walked to a nearby park and all the children experienced such joy to see parts of Romania they had never before seen except from the barred windows.

Just when we children were experiencing a change for the better, for some others it got worse because they turned eighteen years old and knew they had to transfer to the Old Men's Home. They didn't want to go, but there was no other option for them. They were moved to another kind of warehouse for humans.

Most of the children who lived in the hospital weren't capable enough to live on their own or on the streets. I think that putting them in the old folk's home was the next best thing for their care. Some orphanages will just throw the eighteen-year-olds out on the streets. At least the ones who had formerly lived at the Camin Spital, still had a roof over their heads and a place where they could be safe.

~~~~~~~~~~~~~~~~~~~~~~~~~~~~~~~

## Chapter Ten

### Mothers Day, May, 1990

Our house nannies Dina, Emilia, Ildi, Marina, Olga, Dana, and Florica began teaching us some songs, preparing us for Mother's Day. For the first time in our lives, we would perform a concert in front of our parents, the house nannies and some government officials.

As one might expect, all the songs were dedicated to mothers. We practiced many times until we memorized them. We had to also practice getting on stage until we knew our places without mistakes or falling down. After weeks and months went by, we finally learned the songs and our positions on stage.

Still it hurt me to sing some of the words taught to us by Dina and Emilia because I had no mother. "Next to you, Mother, I will sit close to you, I am found, my dear mother, it's the greatest thing to have happened in my life."

When Mother's Day arrived, we got up, bathed and dressed in really nice clothes (donated to us from the Germans and the Dutch). At 9:00 a.m., before we performed, Livia, our teacher, came in with flowers and a card for every child to give to her/his mother. It seemed such a cruel joke to play on orphans with no mothers! Some of us asked if our parents were going to be there for sure. I even asked if my mother was going to come and see me?

"Izidor, your mother will be here to see you today," Livia promised.

Then we began singing. All the house nannies came to watch us, even the ones who were off duty. As we performed, I looked around for my mother. I'm sure I wasn't the only one looking. I don't really know why I looked when I didn't know my parents or how they looked.

I had been right from the beginning; the promise that my mother would come to see me was a cruel, monstrous joke. But it was not so funny for a small nine-year old abandoned boy!

Not one of our parents came to see us, not one mother came to see her child! When we finished singing, we gave the Mother's Day cards and the flowers to the house nannies and to the Dutch. I gave mine to Ildi, since she was one of my favorite house nannies. Christina also gave her card to Ildi.

After everyone left, we replaced our nice clothes with the old clothes we wore every day. Later, Christina and I went home with Ildi. She had two children, Diana and Christian, but everyone called him Ryan. He and I had great fun laying a plan to tease the little girls, chasing them around the house, pulling at their pigtails and making awful monster faces to make them scream.

Diana ran down the hall, squealing, "I hate you, I hate you, Izidor," and I laughed at her, knowing I was tormenting her. My determination to tease her unmercifully also helped to ease the pain of my recent disappointment.

Christina also tried to escape from Ryan's "attention," but he managed to jump from the closet and scare her almost to tears with his loud roar. I nudged Ryan in the side and we both laughed in great satisfaction for a job well done.

Finally, Ildi said "*enough*!" and we all went outdoors to play with a group of kids who looked very familiar to me. I recognized them from years ago when I hung out with them at Onisa's house. They even remembered me! Onisa must have lived nearby Ildi, but I wasn't sure, so I left it alone.

Christina and I especially had fun playing outside till dinner. A feeling of freedom filled our souls. Ildi cooked us French-fries the Romanian way with heavy salt and oil. French-fries and *Sarmale* (Cabbage roll) are my favorites. During the evening we watched television before bedtime. In the morning, we had to return to the hospital, but we didn't want to go back. We begged to stay but had to return. I loved being in a real home.

Onisa had been the first house nanny who took me home with her. Marika was the second who had done so. Later, I had the opportunity to go home with many more house nannies, but no matter how many apartments or homes I visited, it was never the same as Onisa's home. I believe that one of the reasons I loved Onisa's apartment the best was because it was the first home I'd ever seen in all my life.

## Chapter Eleven

### First Christmas in the Hospital

Another season, another reason to learn new songs. This time, we learned Christmas songs, preparing a performance for a large group of visitors, something we had never before done. We practiced long hours until we got it right.

December 25, 1989, the day of our performance, was a big day for everyone. By 10:00 a.m., we took our places on the stage and began singing. When I saw the crowd there to watch us, I could not believe how many people actually showed up -- over 100 people! Not one was a parent. Most who came were members of the Dutch, German and American relief organizations, the Romanian inspection team, and all the house nannies who were scheduled or off-duty -- they all came to see us.

At the end of our performance, we had a surprise that truly shocked us: a Santa Claus came for a Christmas visit. We had reason to be frightened by an entity we'd never before heard of or seen. Santa gave each of us a large sack filled with candy and other goodies. This gift, too, was a shock!

With time, I learned more about Santa Claus, the giver of gifts at Christmas time. After Santa's visit, I went to the window to watch as the people left. I saw two City buses and three vans, filled with laughing, happy people. They must have carried away all the celebration because, later, when another visitor took pictures of us, no one smiled to commemorate our first Christmas in the *Hospital of the Irrecoverable Children*.

One afternoon toward Spring, when nannies Ildi, Dina, Olga and Emilia were scheduled for the afternoon shift, they took us to a different park, one with many more rides and play equipment. We had a lot more fun there. The nannies played with us and taught us new songs. We played so hard that we didn't return to the hospital till after dark. That was another first.

Out of all the hospital nannies, Ildi, Dina, Emilia, Olga, Florica, Marina and Danna had the most respect for children. The work they did to help us learn, take us out for adventures, and the things they did for us was more than any other house nanny had ever done for us. They barely hit us when we did something wrong. Even when they did hit us, it was hard for me to hate them because, most of the time, they were so good to us. They were like a miracle from God to have them work in our hospital. It is because of them that children are living a better life there today.

Looking back with an adult viewpoint I can also see that they had more time to be loving and patient; their workload was often half that of the other nannies.

Here's a little personal description about the nannies from a nine-year old child's perspective. Dina and Emilia were best friends, but acted more like sisters. They always worked the same shift and always got off at the same time. They even looked alike and acted alike. Both women had long black hair. Anytime Dina, Emilia, and Olga were shy or embarrassed; their faces turned bright red. Ildi had a loving heart for the children and treated the children like they were humans, not animals.

On our second year of celebrating Christmas Day, we did another performance and received all kinds of goodies. After the second shift came on duty, Director Viorel invited some of us kids and the first shift nannies to come to his house to sing Christmas carols on his front porch. We left the hospital around three in the afternoon. It was a beautiful day; snow covered the ground and continued falling – large fluffy flakes, beautiful, but dangerous for most of us who had difficulty walking. When we arrived, we knocked and the director and his wife opened the door. We sang the Christmas songs like we were supposed to do but, after finishing the songs, we got another surprise when we were all invited into their home.

Mrs. Viorel had cooked the whole day, waiting for our arrival. The house nannies and the director ate in one room, and we ate in a different room, watching color television for the first time. His wife checked on us every few minutes, seeing how we were doing and if we needed anything else to eat. Viorel even came into the room and talked with us. His home was very beautiful and, in many ways, it looked like Onisa's apartment.

Director Viorel was very kind to the children, but he was not a pleasant person to deal with if you worked at the hospital. However, I discovered if you really got to know him, then you could get along with him just fine, so long as you didn't piss him off! I liked the director because he asked us if any of the house nannies beat us. I think he knew which ones beat us and who did not.

To tell you the truth, I think Viorel was the best director over all we'd had in the past. He checked on us and asked us how we were doing. Most of the other directors didn't even bother to check our living conditions. Although Viorel had a drinking problem – you could smell the alcohol on his breath and the house nannies often gossiped about how he was often drunk on the job -- and he chain-smoked cigarettes, he was still a good director for the children. Again, from an adult viewpoint, I can see how his frustration at being able to help us more, may have caused him to drink to dull those feelings.

Viorel had two children, Viorel, Jr. and Mariana. I got to be pretty good friends with his son. Once his son even signed me out of the hospital and took me home with him for a few hours where we watched that great color television set.

During summer Viorel and his wife took a two-week vacation to Holland, paid for by a group of Dutch missionaries who had worked at the hospital for a year or more. When he returned, he came back with a Volkswagen, a gift to him from the Dutch. I never quite understood why he got such a grand gift, but I wondered if they gave it to him so they could get more children adopted by Dutch couples. It's another mystery to me.

Viorel and each Dutch Relief group got along very well while they stayed in Romania to work with the children. Each month, a new group would arrive. Pete, one of the Dutchmen, was the one who had originally come up with the idea of volunteering at the hospital.

One summer afternoon, Director Viorel had a meeting with the house nannies about some changes in operations. House nannies would now be assigned to work on different floors with different children. The meeting began at 3:00 p.m. and the Dutch were there, as well, because they had come to visit the children.

During the meeting, there was supposed to be one house nanny on each floor taking care of the children. Instead, the house nanny on my floor put me in charge and she went to the meeting so she wouldn't miss anything. I knew that the Dutch were going to come to our floor to see us. Before they came, I told all the kids that they needed to be on their best behavior and not to jump into their arms. They always did that, trying to get more attention.

"If any of you jumps into their arms and doesn't listen to me, then I will beat you after the Dutch leave this room," I threatened.

Ten minutes later, the Dutch came on our floor, and the first thing all the kids did was get up from their seats and jump into their arms! I tried to get the kids to stop, but they wouldn't listen to me. Oh, I was angry! So now I would punish them, just as the nannies punished us all. Shortly after they left, I had my friend Anita pull out a chair and put it in the middle where all the kids could see it. I laid one child over the seat, pulled down his pants and beat his butt with my shoes, while two other kids held him down so he couldn't get away from me.

Every kid who did not listen to me received a beating. After I hit a few kids, they all settled down. Once I got them to listen to me, I had things under control again. I had to let them know I was the boss for now and they had to do what I told them to do. If they didn't listen to what I said, then another beating was given out by me. I did exactly as the nannies did to control us. Once I regained control, I had the kids sing songs and we played games. An hour later, the meeting ended and every house nanny came back to her post, crying. Most of them got transferred to a different floor.

Felicia, the evil one, was assigned to our floor. They reassigned Dana to work with the 18-year-old girls, but she didn't want to leave us. She cried and cried, asking the director for mercy to let her stay, but he would not allow it, so a group of us begged him to let her stay with us and he finally gave in and said yes. Dana, Emilia, Florica, Olga and Marina remained with us, which was good. I would have cried my head off if they had been moved from our floor. The rest, we didn't really care about, just so long as he didn't move the good ones. As for Ildi, we wanted to get her back, but she wanted to work on a different floor. My friend Christina and I both cried because we loved Ildi and wanted her to work with us.

That night, after putting all the kids to bed, Tibi showed me a watch he had under his bed. I asked him where he got it?

"I stole it from the Dutch when they came in this afternoon," he replied.

I didn't say anything to the house nanny because I knew I would be blamed for it anyway. That night, all the kids from all the floors had to sleep out in the hallways because the bedrooms were sprayed for bugs.

The next day, the Dutch and the director came up on my floor, asking about the watch. The first people they asked were Marian, Tibi, Anita, Janna, Christina and me. Quickly, before they checked the beds, I went into my room to get my coins given to me by a house nanny and hidden beneath my mattress. One of the nannies saw me and reported me to the group.

"Izidor has the watch," she said. "He stole it."

I tried to explain myself, but they didn't believe a word I said. Eventually, they found the watch on Marin's wrist. I don't know how he got hold of it. After the group left, we were surprised that we weren't in more trouble; for punishment, they only made us kneel for two hours with our arms held over our heads. It wasn't so bad. After a little while you don't even feel the hard concrete, you just get sort of numb.

Just a few weeks later, someone stole a can of coffee from the Dutch supplies, but this time it was one of the house nannies. No one knew for sure who stole the coffee, but the director made the rule very clear.

"If you don't find that coffee within an hour, then you're all fired," he said.

The coffee was found soon after but no one was fired because they never did find out who stole the coffee.

Not long after the incident with the coffee, someone stole more than one-hundred dollars that belonged to one of the house nannies. Can you guess who was blamed for her money being stolen? Yes, we children were blamed for it once again. Anita, Marin, Christina, Tibi and I were the chosen "guilty" ones.

"If the money isn't returned by five this evening, then we will call the police and report you," proclaimed the director. "If the police come here, they will cut off your hands and will take you to jail. In jail the police will beat you with a belt."

We shook with fright when he told us that, because we didn't want to lose our hands or go to prison. Terrified, some of us threw up, some of us cried and some of us ran to the bathroom to relieve ourselves. No one would believe our innocence. By three in the afternoon the money was still missing and things looked bad for us. Over and over we wailed that we didn't steal the money. Moments later, a house nanny came in with a long, sharp butcher knife.

"Okay, if you don't tell us who stole the money we are going to cut off your hands," she hissed, making rapid chopping motions in the air in front of our saucer-round eyes.

We clung to one another and I screamed with terror when she grabbed my hand and used the dull side of the knife, pretending to cut off my hand.

"Wait, I know who stole the money," shouted Tibi, trying to save me. "It was Anglika!"

He blamed the theft on one of the mean house nannies, who hated us and always called us gypsies. When she was confronted by the other women, she was angry and wanted to know who blamed her for stealing the money.

"Who said this?" she screamed. "One of the gypsy kids? You know they lie and steal all the time. Tell me who said it and I'll get the truth," she promised.

Lucky for us, the house nanny who had her money stolen, believed our side of the story more than she did the one we accused. The money was never found, but once we blamed it on someone else, we were off the hook.

The local police investigated the woman we accused but never found any money on her. She wasn't fired, but was I glad we weren't punished for that damage! The smarter ones among us were always blamed for something that was stolen or broken. Yes, most of the time we were the ones to cause the damage and steal things from visitors and the house nannies but, sometimes, we were wrongfully accused, and then we still received punishment. It didn't seem fair to us.

## Chapter Twelve

### More donations

More donations came to us from Holland; three huge trucks of supplies. The Dutch kept track of everything donated to the children. Among the gifts were a television set and a bike. When I saw the television, I vowed to get it placed on the third floor before someone could take it home with them. It took over three hours to unload all the trucks. One-half was going to be donated to an orphanage not far from our hospital.

Just a few days later, the house nannies started to sort out the clothes for the children but, this time, the director would not allow anyone to take things home. However, for some people, there is always a way, usually by using us, the kids.

I went downstairs to see what kinds of things had been donated, but one house nanny asked me to put on a sweater and take a stuffed animal upstairs. The director, smart to their ways now, asked them if someone was going to take the sweater and toy away from me once he left. I told him they had given them to me. I thought it was true, but by the time the three o'clock shift came on duty, my sweater and the stuffed animal were taken by one of the nannies. The director never even asked me what had happened to my things. Even he could not fight against the poverty of the workers.

As for the television, one of the cooks asked the director if he could take the television home with him. When I heard him asking for the television, I went down to Viorel's office and asked him for the fourth time when he was going to put the television on my floor.

"Did one of the house nannies put you up to this?" Viorel asked me.

"No," I lied. "They don't even know I came here."

"Okay," he said, "I'll have the television brought up there in few minutes."

I thanked him and left his office. The truth was, I was sent by the nannies to ask Viorel for the television. They knew I had a better chance of getting a favor from him. He kept his word and the television was brought up ten minutes later. The house nannies knew what they were doing; they knew I got along well with the director.

Our floor became famous for the television set. Nobody had ever seen one before. I think it also made the nannies' job easier; we'd sit for hours, hypnotized, watching the black and white pictures flicker and flash across the small screen. It was like magic!

A few weeks later, the director had another meeting about switching people around. I don't know why he kept doing it. Some nannies said it was so he could have more control, while others claimed they were punished for having favorites. This time, evil Felicia was put in charge on my floor. No one liked her because she was so mean to us. Even the other nannies feared her.

When all the other nannies left, I told Tibi to throw a fork at Felicia. He did, and Felicia saw him. She walked over to my friend and slapped him across the face. When Tibi got slapped, everyone started laughing, finding it funny, so I threw a spoon at Felicia and she slapped me, as well. Someone else told Tibi to hit Felicia in the stomach. Brave (or stupid) poor Tibi walked up to her and punched her as hard as he could. Angry now, Felicia got the broomstick and hit Tibi and a few of the other kids as hard as she could.

It was always the same. Felicia took our fights like a man. It never hurt her when Tibi punched her. She still had the strength to hit us back harder than we could hit her. Eventually, she won that round and we stopped fighting so she had things back under control before the other house nannies could see us hit Felicia, or her hitting us back. By the time they returned, we were all sitting, watching television again.

More changes were made. Ildi came back to work on the third floor with us. Felicia was moved to the fourth floor to work with the 18-year-old boys. We celebrated because we thought the fights would be more even with the older boys. We believed that the director had put Felicia there because he knew how abusive she was with us.

The next day Felicia called in sick and said she didn't feel so good. When we heard that Felicia was sick, I was happy, because I knew that we did hurt her after all. Having Felicia working on the fourth floor with the big boys was punishment for her because those kids sure did hit her a lot. Most of the boys on that floor were violent and had seizures and epilepsy.

### Saturday and Sunday

On Saturday and Sundays routines were different then they were during the week. All the teachers and aids were off on the weekend. Dina, Emilia, Mariana, Dana, Florica, Olga and Ildi were assistant teachers at the hospital and were always off then.

When the teachers and their assistants were not on duty, the house nannies allowed me to be in charge of all the kids on my section of the floor, between 50 and 60 children my age and younger. I wasn't always allowed to be in charge when the teachers worked because the house nannies feared they'd report it to the director. Kids were never supposed to be in charge of other kids, especially one like me who was only nine years old, but as long as the director didn't know, then it was fine with the house nannies. It saved them work.

Here is how I did things when I was in charge of the kids on my floor.

Rodica might come on duty at three in the afternoon and ask if I wanted to be in charge of all the kids. "I don't feel good today," she would say. "You be in charge."

Sometimes I would be allowed to take the children outside to play. Usually I didn't care what the children did outside as long as they were on their best behavior and listened to what I told them. When it was time to go back upstairs for dinner, Anita, Jannia, Christina and I fed all the children who were in bed. The ones, who were not in bed, fed themselves.

After dinner we bathed the children before putting them to bed. When they were ready for bed and all cleaned up, we allowed them to watch a television show called *Dallas*, an American series that was aired on the Romanian television every Sunday evening at eight o'clock. All the house nannies who worked Sunday night came on our floor to watch that show, too. It was the most popular program on television back then, I guess in the whole world.

Just watching *Dallas* and seeing what America looked like, I really wanted to go there to see for myself. After the show was over we put all the kids to bed. If there was nothing else for me to do, I would sit in the nurse's office with the house nanny, chatting away, waiting for the nine o'clock shift to come on duty.

The following week, I was put in charge of the kids on my floor once again, but this time it was in the morning. They behaved well so we played games and sang songs. For some reason, at lunchtime, not all the kids wanted to eat their meal. I told the kids, "If you eat your lunch, then you'll all grow big and strong." They believed me and ate their lunch. I don't know where I learned this psychology at age nine, certainly not from the nannies!

We had *Sarmale* (cabbage rolls) and potato soup. All the kids ate all their food and there wasn't anything left in the cooking pots. When the nannies came to see how I was doing and if I needed any help feeding the children, they were surprised to see that the soup pot and *Sarmale* pot were completely empty. They couldn't believe the children ate all their food; usually there were leftovers that were fed to the pigs kept outside in front of the hospital. I think all the kids needed was someone to encourage them. When I look back, I guess I was a pretty good boss, even then!

## Chapter Thirteen

### Help from America

January 1990, a group of Americans came to see the children. Before they could see any of us, Director Viorel had the cooks make them something to eat, stalling them from seeing the kids in their bad condition.

**JOHN UPTON**

While the Americans were in his office, he came up on all the floors and told the nannies to make sure all the kids were dressed properly and the place was cleaned up. After delivering his orders, he went back to his office. Within an hour, the Americans came on the third floor, and the first thing we did was singsongs for them. It was something we always had to do when anyone came from a different country. By doing so, it seemed like life was not so bad at the hospital.

The people who came to our hospital that day were John (American), Anna (Canadian) and Anca, Marius and Elena (Romanian translators). At first, everyone thought that John and his group had come to the hospital only to see us kids, like all the others. Then word spread that the Americans were in Romania to take children to the United States of America for medical treatment. Everyone was surprised to hear that.

Every day, John visited us in the hospital and played with us. We kids grew to love John, but we always called him Johnny instead. He stayed in Romania for a month, looking for the parents of many of the children he wanted to take to America. In order for Johnny to take any child out of Romania, he had to first get authorization from the child's parent and from the Romanian Government.

**JOHNNY FROM AMERICA**

Within a few weeks, Johnny chose which children he would take to America for medical treatment. He arranged a meeting with these children in the director's office. The children chosen were: Izabela, Christina, Chiprian, Christian, Elena, Anna and me, Izidor.

Since she was a baby, Izabela was paralyzed in both her legs. She never received therapy or the opportunity to learn to walk while in the hospital, but only lay in bed for seventeen years. According to the Romanian doctors, Izabela could never learn how to walk so, since the doctor had made his decision, Izabela was

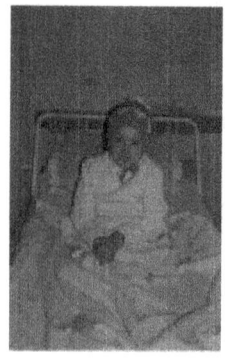

**IZABELA, AGE 17 YEARS**

never taught how to walk. I wondered if there was hope if she traveled to America for treatment?

Christina was blind in her left eye. Her left eye was light blue and her right eye was dark blue. She was able to see out of her dark blue eye. Treatment in America could repair the damage to her left eye, although being blind in one eye had never stopped Christina from doing anything that she wanted to do in life.

Anna was completely blind in both eyes. She was born blind, but she was a smart girl nevertheless.

Chiprian had a speech problem and was slow in catching on to things. Today, you would call him a slow learner. Chiprian was born with a speech problem and fetal alcohol syndrome, also known as FAS.

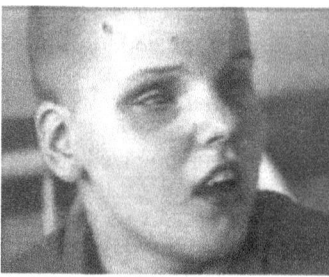

**ANNA, AGE 15 YEARS**

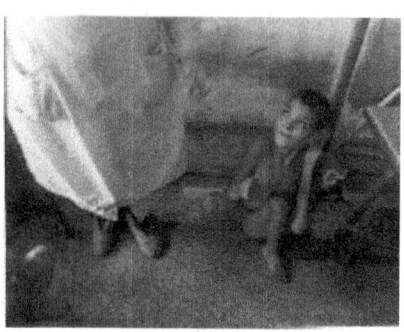

**ELENA, AGE 12 YEARS**

Elena had a terrible birth defect; she was born with one leg twisted and bent over her shoulder. She could not walk. Instead, she dragged along on the filthy rough concrete floor, on her bare butt to move around. You see, no one ever tried to make clothes to fit her deformed body, so she lived nude her whole life.

I was born with a disability that no one seemed to be able to diagnose, but my legs were crippled and Johnny told me I could have an operation to fix them.

The first time he called us to the director's office, I thought I was going to have an operation right then. I was so scared and so were all the other kids in that office. One of the reasons I had thought I was going to have an operation in the director's office was because of the video camera Johnny carried with him. I had never seen a video camera so, therefore, I thought the camera was a machine to use for the operation and I was afraid.

All Johnny really wanted to do was to catalog our disabilities. After he examined us, we all went back upstairs. Everyone talked about how some of us were going to America. It was the news of the month in the hospital.

Some of the house nannies didn't want us to go and some did. The second time Johnny saw us, it looked like Christina and I

**CHOOSING THE CHILDREN FOR AMERICA**

were going to be the first children to go to America. When the nannies realized that Christina and I were going to be the first ones to leave, they broke into tears, especially Ildi, Emilia and Dina. Ildi loved Christina and me, and she did not want to lose us and never see us again. Christina and I were both very excited about going to America, but she tried to frighten us so we wouldn't go. She said the Americans weren't going to help us, that they were going to use our body parts to fix only American children. It didn't work.

On Johnny's third visit, he came to see all the children on my floor. Making the best of the situation, Ildi wanted Johnny to see how Christina had learned to do gymnastics. She wanted Johnny to know that Christina was smarter than she looked, although she was blind in one eye. Other than that, she was fine.

Within a week, Johnny and Anca came on my floor with the camera to videotape all the children. Dina and Emilia were scheduled to work that afternoon. As Johnny and Anca set up their camera, I went to see Johnny. Emilia tried to stop me, but Johnny said I could stay with him. One by one, he called to each child. He asked them their name and their age. Some children could not speak or would not speak, so he asked Dina and Emilia if they knew their names and how old they were. Dina and Emilia didn't know most of the children's last name or their ages so Dina asked me if I knew.

It's a good thing that Johnny told them to let me stay in that room because I knew every child's first and last name. It even shocked Johnny and the nannies that I knew everyone's name so well. How could I not know everyone's name when I had been living in that hospital for more than ten years?

After Johnny was done filming the other children, he asked me to come and sit on his lap. I got up and limped towards him, then sat on his lap. "Izidor, don't you want to play soccer with the American kids?" he asked.

"Yes," I replied, "I want to play soccer with the American kids, but I am scared of the operation."

"If you don't want the operation, then you don't have to have it," he promised.

I felt much better that I actually had a choice about the operation.

Within a few days, Johnny came back with a child's mother, which meant that one of us was going to America. The question was who was going to America? That's what we were all wondering. It wasn't too long before we found out. It was my friend Anna, the girl who was blind since birth, but very smart. When someone sang her a song the first time, she knew the song by the second time. For most of us, we had to hear the song over and over before we learned it, but Anna only had to hear it once.

By 3:00 p.m., Johnny and his crew came on my floor to pick up Anna. It was time to leave. They took her downstairs to the waiting car. All the children rushed to the windows, crying and heartbroken that we were left behind. When the car pulled away, we all called good bye as we cried and stuck our hands between the window bars, waving farewell.

Feeling our hearts breaking, every child shouted, "Johnny, take me to America," but Johnny only smiled sadly and waved back as he drove away from the hospital. We were left behind, hopeless, and we knew we would never see Johnny again. I watched the car until it disappeared from view, knowing I was never going to America. That day it was all I could think about: Anna was gone and I was stuck here. And yet, I was happy for her. In America she would be able to see!

For weeks, all everyone talked about was how Anna went to America. It wasn't too long before rumors started spreading that the Americans killed Anna to use her body parts. From that day on, none of the house nannies liked the idea of the other children going to America. They didn't trust Johnny anymore, they said. I knew, if Johnny did come back to take more children to America, the house nannies could not really do anything about it. It was up to the biological parents and the government, whether they would allow more children to leave Romania.

A few months later, Johnny returned. He had come to take more children to America. Cergei, the Romanian translator, told me I was going to America for sure this time. I believed Cergei and I was filled with joy once more. I hoped this time I really would have the opportunity to get out of the hospital.

Some weeks later, another American came to adopt a child from the hospital. Her name was Ann, and she was there to adopt Calin. Calin hadn't been living in the hospital his whole life. From what I heard, he came to the *Camin Spital* because his father was very abusive to him and the rest of the family so they decided to put him here for his own protection.

I could not believe it! Was Calin better off living in the hospital then at home with his own family? I knew it could not be true because every child put into the hospital or an orphanage would eventually get abused anyway.

Calin was slow in his mind and had a speech problem. That was his only disability. Ann came to the hospital almost every day. When she came to see him, all the other kids wanted attention, too. I don't think Ann wanted to give everyone that attention because she'd take Calin into a different room where they didn't have to be around all the other kids jumping all over Ann. I suppose it was understandable because she wanted to get to know her new child.

On one of her visits, many of us were playing outdoors. Ann decided to come out with Calin to see what we did. Tibia and I went behind her and started going through her purse. We found two rolls of film. We had hoped we could find some American money in her purse, but before we could look deeper, nanny Marina caught us and we had to give back the two rolls of film that we took. Marina introduced herself to Ann and they began speaking French. Ann told Marina that there would be two more Americans coming to the hospital to adopt Chiprian and me.

Sure enough, it happened as Ann said it would. Later, Marika walked on my floor with two Americans. Marika called out, "Chiprian and Izidor, come here. The Americans are here to see you."

As soon as the tall woman saw us, she broke into tears. Marlys was the tall American, and Debbie was the short American. They had two translators with them, Roxana and Calin, a married couple. We went into the nurse's office to speak privately without all the house nannies listening to what we were saying, but they ended up being in the office, too.

Marlys could not stop crying. "Roxana, why is the tall American crying?" I asked.

"Because she is very happy she has finally found you," she said, smiling at the woman. "Izidor, why don't you hug her to make her feel better?"

When I knelt to hug Marlys she began to cry even more, not knowing that Roxana had asked me to hug her.

Debbie held Chiprian in her arms as Chiprian rummaged through her purse, seeing if she had any candy for him.

"Izidor, do you want to go to America?" Marlys asked.

The only thing I could say was, "Yes!" I was so excited and full of joy to hear that someone actually wanted to take me to America. "Roxana, which one is going to be my new mother," I asked.

"Which one do you want to have as your mother?"

"Which is my mother?" I begged to know.

"The tall American is your new mother," she replied.

"Then that's who I want to have as my mother," I said. When I picked Marlys, she began to cry, filled with joy to see that I had picked her.

We talked with Marlys and Debbie for at least an hour before they had to leave. I asked my new mother if she would come back tomorrow.

"Yes, we will be back tomorrow to see you both," said Marlys.

"When will you come?"

"We will be back around 8:00 in the morning," she promised.

When they left the building, I went to the window to watch the two women as they walked away. When I went to have my lunch, I noticed that Dina and Emilia were crying. When I saw people crying that I loved, sometimes I cried with them. That's what I did when I saw them crying. I knew they would miss me and I was going to miss them the most. Everyone believed that Chiprian and I would leave the hospital very soon. Most of the house nannies gave me their address so I could write to them from America.

The next morning, I went to the window watching for Marlys and Debbie. As the minutes ticked by, I didn't see them and my heart sank. After an hour of waiting, I gave up and thought to myself, "They're not coming to see us." My heart ached and I began to build a thick wall around it so it wouldn't break.

Before lunchtime, they did come after all and they brought some candy for us this time: Still, I was wary of their promise. They were not allowed to come upstairs because the director was not in his office. Instead we were taken downstairs to them. We went into an office to speak privately with the Americans. Some house nannies stood at the door, listening, to see if I would say anything bad about them. Roxana got up and closed the door so no one could hear our conversation.

"Izidor, do the house nannies ever hit you?" Roxana asked.

I didn't say anything. She promised me that she would never tell anyone. "Yes, they hit us sometimes when we don't listen to them."

Since Chiprian and I could not sign our names, they fingerprinted us. Marlys and Debbie measured our shoe size and discussed the size of our clothing. After our meeting, we went back upstairs to have lunch with the rest of the kids. We felt such excitement that we could barely eat our food. Was I really going to America? *Careful*, warned my heart.

A few days later, I went to the window to see who would work the afternoon shift. I noticed a man walk right through the gate. I had never seen him before. The stranger carried a sack on his shoulder and looked dirty, as if he was homeless. The next thing I knew, one of the nannies called out my name.

"Izidor, your father is here to see you."

"What? My father?" I exclaimed. "I have no father."

Ignoring my protestations, the house nannies on my floor checked if I looked clean and was dressed properly. When I went down to see my so-called father, it was the guy I'd seen from the window, the one who looked so dirty.

Director Viorel invited my father and me into his office. One of the director's first questions to the man was, "What made you come all of sudden?"

I don't remember my father's response exactly, but he said he heard that Americans wanted to adopt me and he didn't want that to happen; he would take me back home now. He opened the dirty sack and pulled out huge size clothes and man sized shoes. The director couldn't believe that my own father didn't know my age and how big I was. He must have imagined me to be much older, but I had just turned eleven years old at the time and only weighed about fifty pounds. Children who lived at the hospital didn't get enough food to grow normally.

My father wanted to take me home with him that very day, but the director told him he had to first have my mother and him sign all the forms for my release. My father told him he would be back later. After he left, Viorel poured himself a drink from the bottle in his desk, and I went to the window and waited for my parents to return for me. I waited for hours and hours, but they never came back for me that day.

I was angry and confused because my father had lied to me; he did not come back for me like he said he would. On top of it all, Marlys and Debbie hadn't come back to the hospital to see Chiprian and me for weeks. What was going to happen to me? As I wondered, the wall around my heart hardened.

Three days later, my father, mother, big brother, and baby sister came. My parent's names were Maria and Izidor Bojani. I was named after my father! My brother was Mugurel and my baby sister was Onisa. I smiled when I heard her name and I wanted to hold her, but I knew I wasn't strong enough. She had just been born a week before my father came for me.

This time, they brought my favorite drink, *suke* (which is tart lemonade), cake and bread. After we ate, the director invited us all into his office to speak about me leaving the hospital. Viorel said he did not have a problem with me going home with them. All my parents had to do was fill out the paperwork and return it to him when he came back from his lunch. While my parents were filling out the forms, Mugurel and I went upstairs to eat lunch with all the other kids. He was scared of some of them and couldn't stop staring at my friends like they were freaks or something.

The house nannies said that Mugurel looked just like me, both of us, gypsies. When we finished our lunch, we went back downstairs to see if my parents had finished filling out the paperwork. Sure enough, they were done. Now we could only wait for the director to return.

Soon nanny Reghina gave me a board game and a German jacket to take home with me. While we waited, I took them downstairs in the hallway. The Dutch volunteers and the house nannies kept walking by to look at my parents.

My mother asked one of the Dutch volunteers about the lady who wanted to adopt me. "Who is she?" my mother asked. "Why does she want to adopt my son?"

"To give him a better life in America," he replied.

After waiting a few hours, Viorel returned. He said he'd changed his mind about letting me go home with my birth parents.

My mother lost her temper. "Mr. Director, why can't I take my son home? Why are you stopping us?"

It seemed that the more questions my mother asked, the angrier the director got with her. At one point, he raised his hand as if he might hit her, but he controlled himself. "You don't want your son back because you love him," he shouted. "You only came here when you heard about a rich American who wanted to adopt Izidor. You only want to sell him to her for money, you greedy woman."

He threw open the office door and glared at my parents. "Get out of my hospital. Get out of my sight, and never come here again," he ordered. "Izidor is not going anywhere with you. Get out!"

With my baby sister crying, my parents and brother hurriedly left without me, and that was the last time I saw them. Two visits, and that was it. I was abandoned for life all over again.

Looking back, it seems to me that the director didn't want me to go home with my birth parents because he believed they would put me on the streets to beg for money. Many kids who were taken out of the hospital by their birth parents did end up being put on the streets. In my opinion, Viorel was only protecting me, and I am grateful to him.

Since I couldn't go home with my parents, the director asked one of the workers to take me for a bike ride to make me feel better. That didn't make me feel better at all. Since I didn't go home with my parents, I asked the director if he would allow me to go home with a house nanny that night. He allowed me to go home with Rodica. I'm sure the director would have allowed me to go home with any of the house nannies as long as I was back in the hospital, in his care, the next day.

That night, we left after her shift. It was hard for me to walk to her house because of the disability I had. When I got to Rodica's house, she made me something to eat, then we watched television before bed. For me, it was a long, sad night.

Later, back at the hospital, after supper and baths, all the children were put to bed. Before anyone could fall asleep, three large trucks of donations arrived. Since all the house nannies went to help unload the trucks, we children watched from the windows.

Soon after, nanny Viorica came upstairs with two large bags of plastic balls for us. She knew we were awake, watching as they unloaded the trucks. I was put in charge of the kids on my floor, since there wasn't anyone else to watch them. The unloading went on for hours before they left the orphanage. Most of the kids stayed awake to play with the plastic balls, their first toy.

By midnight, everyone went to sleep. In the middle of the night, I felt someone sitting on my leg. I woke up to see who was sitting on my bed. It was Viorica, but she told me to go back to sleep. When we woke in the morning, we discovered nannies from the night shift had stolen the balls while we were sleeping.

When Viorica sat on my leg in the middle of the night, she meant to sit on the edge of the bed to get the ball that I had hidden under my bed. When things got stolen from us, there wasn't anything we could do to get it back. Good things went to the house nannies and the poor things went to us. That's how it worked with the donations.

As weeks went by, Marlys and Debbie returned to see Chiprian and me, but because the director was not at the hospital, they could not get past the gate. Roxana finally talked the guard into letting them inside the gate to see us.

I asked Marlys if I could take some pictures of Dina and Emilia, since they were standing next to us. She gave me her camera and allowed me to take a few pictures. Before they left, I gave her a pair of sunglasses that Dina and Emilia had bought for me when they took me to the store. Then they were gone, perhaps for the last time, and the wall grew higher around my heart.

I did not know until later, that the two women had stayed in Romania for six more weeks, trying to find our biological parents, to ask them for authorization to allow us to go to America. Neither Chiprin nor my parents could be found. Marlys hired the *Satu-Mare* Police Department to locate my parents. The police told her that my parents were in jail for stealing. When she went to the jail she discovered they had been released a few days before.

Because our parents could not be found, the whole adoption procedure turned into a court trial. The court trail went on for fifteen days and our parents never came to one court trial. Therefore, the judge could make a ruling on whether he would allow Chiprian and me to go to America.

I found out later that, during one of the trial days, my birth mother came to Marlys' attorney and asked if she could speak with her. "No, you may not speak with Marlys if you are going to try to get money from her," said the attorney. My biological mother left, once the attorney said that she could not ask for money. Now the way was clear for Chiprian and me to go to America. Or so I thought.

## Chapter Fourteen

### Third child gone to America

One afternoon, Calin came back to the hospital to bring another child with him to America. Calin was Marlys' translator when she first came to see me. The girl chosen now to go to America was Izabela, my teenage friend who had spent her life in bed. She was the third child to leave. My hopes were once again dashed. I felt like I would never get out of that hospital.

Before Calin left, he came upstairs to see Chiprian and me and to give us a message from Marlys and Debbie. They wanted us to know they were not giving up and that we were coming to America soon. They gave Calin a bag of candy for each of us. I broke into tears when I found out for sure that I was being left behind for the third time.

Before Izabela left the hospital, I went downstairs to say good bye to her. Her grandmother was with her in the car. We all watched as they drove off. In my mind, I thought that I would never have the opportunity to go to America. I pretty much gave up and I threw away all the addresses the house nannies had given me. So far, Anna, Calin and Izabela had escaped the hospital. They were on their way to America. I felt like I would never again see Marlys, Debbie or John, and I put a strong lock on the door to my heart as I tried to protect myself from more pain.

## Chapter Fifteen

### Going home with Dina

One summer night, nanny Dina wanted to take me home with her. After her shift ended at 8:00 p.m. we went home. As we walked with Emilia, Florica and Marina past a church, I saw a big statue of a man nailed to a cross.

I asked Dina, "Who is that person on the cross?"

"That is Mr. Jesus Christ," Dina said.

"Why is he on that cross?" I asked.

"Because Christ died for people like you and me."

I didn't understand what Dina meant, so I left it alone. When we got to her house, we all split up and went our own ways. Marina lived right across the street from Dina. Emilia lived just a few houses down. Florica lived several blocks up the street.

For supper Dina cooked me French fries, my favorite. Afterward, we went to Emilia's house to see her sister and her brother. We sat outside, visiting, just talking about life. I made-believe I lived with Dina in a normal home in a normal neighborhood like a normal little boy. It felt wonderful to share an evening with friends, with no fear of beatings. After our visit, Dina and I went back home to sleep.

In the morning after my breakfast, I asked Dina if I could visit Marina.

"Sure, just look in both directions before you cross the street."

When I got to Marina's house, she was cleaning. Then I had another new experience: I helped milk the cow! I even drank the milk, still warm, but very rich tasting.

Later, Emilia and Dina took me swimming at the lake. I didn't know how to swim so Dina gave me an inner tube to hang onto. I held tight because I knew my legs wouldn't help me if I slipped off. The girls teased me they were going to take the tube and make me swim, but they were only kidding. I had fun being at Dina's house. I knew what it felt like to be free.

When we got back to the hospital, kids were running all over the place, screaming and yelling.

"Everyone shut up now," shouted Dina. "If you are all good for the next twenty minutes, we are going to go to the park."

The kids stopped instantly so about thirty of us got to go to the park and then to the train station, just to watch the train go by.

The following week Florica took me home with her. I think everyone was trying to help me forget that I had not been chosen for the third time to go to America.

"You can stay at my house for three or four days," she told me.

It was really hard for me to walk to her house because it was all uphill. I kept falling down on my knees. Halfway there she stopped by a friend's home to borrow a bike so she could ride me home, which went much faster. When we got there, she joined her friends doing gardening. Meanwhile, I played with her nephews and then watched a repairman do a job. After he was finished, I asked if he'd give me a ride in his car. I had never before ridden in an automobile. It was really an adventure, driving in that car. Everything went by so fast!

People often broke their word to me and I didn't trust easily, so when Florica said I could stay at her house for a few days, I didn't really believe her. Instead, I went back to Dina's house, hoping I could stay an extra day out of the orphanage. Soon Florica came over, wondering why I had left her house.

"You have to work tomorrow," I said, "and Dina is off and I wanted to stay home a bit longer."

"Izidor, I said you could stay at my house for three or four days with my nephews and my friends," she said. " I have visitors from France and I wanted you to meet them."

After Florica explained, I knew she had been telling me the truth. I felt really bad and wished I had stayed, but I never went back. Instead, I stayed with Dina for the rest of the night and just went back to the hospital the next morning. Staying with Dina was a sure thing for me. It made such a difference, to be away from that hospital.

Other times Onisa and Marika took me home with them and soon everyone took turns. I probably went home with at least twenty house nannies, all of them with kind hearts. I know they tried to help me forget my three disappointments about going to America. Still, I always remembered the first home I'd seen, and when I have a place of my own, I plan on having my house look just like Onisa's home.

~~~~~~~~~~~~~~~~~~~~~~~~

# Chapter Sixteen

## The Day Finally Arrives

October 8, 1991 arrived the same as usual, get up, eat and bathe. After breakfast, we went outside to play. Nanny Olga got the bike that the Dutch had donated to the children, so we could ride it around the hospital building.

After everyone got the chance to ride, I told Tibi to take the bike and ride it around by himself. When he came back, Marian took the bike and, finally, I took a ride. When I came back, the bike was taken away and we were told to go inside for lunch. When we got upstairs, Dina and Emilia grabbed the broomstick and hit us for not listening to them. We three boys were in shock; it was the first time they'd beaten us. Afterward they felt very guilty.

After lunch, we were put into a schoolroom and told to put our heads on our arms to nap. I sat very still because I didn't want to get into trouble again. Ten minutes before the second shift came on duty; Reghina walked in with Anca, the translator, and called out our names. My heart sank. Was I in trouble again?

"Chiprian, Izidor, come here," she said.

I rose slowly from my chair. What had I done now? When I went to her side she reached for me, and I covered my head to protect myself, but she laughed at me.

"I'm not going to beat you," she said. " You and Chiprian are going to America today."

Everyone woke up when Reghina made that announcement. Going to America? Could it be true? Fearing another heartbreak, I decided that I would believe it when it happened, and not one minute sooner!

Chiprain and I were taken to separate rooms to change our clothes. I didn't like the clothes I had, and I looked over to see if Chiprain had any better clothes, but we both had the same. The house nannies helped us dress quickly; soon the director would return from his lunch. Before we left the third floor, I stopped and took a long look at all the kids for the last time. Even today, I can see each face as we said good bye.

We headed downstairs with Anca to the waiting car. Every house nanny in the building came with us to the car to say good bye. They asked me to write to them and call them once in a while, which shows they didn't know where America was located anymore than I. I told them that I would come back in a helicopter. They all laughed, like that would ever happen. Then they hugged and kissed us one last time.

As we drove from the hospital grounds, the second shift was changing and I rolled down my window to wave good bye. We continued our journey to *Baia-Mare*. From *Maramures* to *Baia-Mare* took about two hour's time. We had lunch there and waited for someone to pick us up at the restaurant to take us to the airport for our flight to *Bucharest*.

When we got on the plane, I was scared for my life because I had never even seen an airplane close up, much less flown on one. I saw one of the flight crew and asked if he could please drive the plane slow. He smiled and said that he would do that.

As the plane started down the runway, I held onto the seat in front of me as hard as I could. Once the plane was airborne, I felt much better. One of the flight crew came to my seat and asked me to come with him. I looked at Anca to see what she would say, but she wanted me to go with him. The man was so kind. He took me into the cockpit to show me how things were controlled. It was amazing! He told me it was safer to fly in the air, rather than drive on the ground. Having had little experience in either case, I was willing to take his word for it!

I spent my time looking out the window at the earth below. Everything looked so small. Around ten o'clock we landed at *Bucharest* and someone met us at the airport to take us home for the night. I stayed with one of Anca's friends and Chiprian stayed with another. The couple I stayed with were very nice and offered me something to eat. I asked for French fries and *suke*. After I ate my supper, I took a bath and went to bed, but I could hardly sleep from the excitement of the trip so far. Was I dreaming, I wondered, or was I really going to America?

In the morning when I woke up, I went to the small balcony to look out over the beautiful capital city of Romania. Everywhere looked I saw construction sites – buildings were going up in every direction, it seemed. It was also noisy outside and crowded with people walking by, but that's what I still remember and love about *Bucharest*, crowded and busy.

The couple's names were Shawnee and Melinda. I missed the chaos of the hospital, but when I felt bored I just looked out the window to see people walk by and the construction going on. They lived on the tenth floor, and that was perfect for me because I loved high buildings where I could see the view from a distance.

The next day, Anca and Chiprian came to Shawnee and Melinda's house. Chiprain had misbehaved badly according to Anca. She wanted me to tell him that he needed to listen to the people that he was staying with, but it was already too late to tell him that, because the lady was not willing to take care of him after the second day so he stayed with me.

Chiprain was good at Melinda's house because I was there with him. He was still scared of me because he knew I would beat him if he did not listen. I stayed with Shawnee and Melinda for three weeks before I was relocated to stay with someone else.

What was taking so long? I wondered. Would they make me return to the hospital? Still unsure and disbelieving, I kept the protective wall around my heart as I bided my time.

I was taken to stay with Marius' mother. Marius and Anca, a married couple, were the translators who had helped the Americans months ago. Now they were hired by Chiprian's and my parents to bring us safely to the United States.

As I told you, Chiprian was born with Fetal Alcohol Syndrome, which caused him to be brain damaged. That was why he misbehaved so much. Fetal Alcohol Syndrome (FAS) is when a woman drinks alcohol while she is pregnant. Most of the times when the child is born, they are sick because of the mother's drinking, and it causes brain damage. That is why a woman should never drink or smoke while pregnant. Although Chiprian had FAS, I don't think that Anca ever could understand his behavior or why he was always so wild. She never had the patience to work with him or with any children that couldn't control their behavior.

I don't know why I was relocated to stay with someone else, but I was. Perhaps the couple couldn't cope with us both. I was even more bored than I was at the high rise. Marius' mother lived in a low building and she didn't have a good view like Melinda and

Shawnee did. As you can see, there wasn't an option of where I could stay.

An eleven-year old orphan on his way to America doesn't get a choice. I tried to make the best of it as they continued cutting through the red tape so I could leave the country.

Marina, Marius' mother, tried to make me feel as comfortable as she could. Don't get me wrong. She was very nice, but it wasn't the same as it was at Melinda's house; every morning waking up and looking out from the balcony, at all the construction and people rushing along. To some people, doing something like that would be boring, but for me it wasn't because there were so many parts of Romania I had never before seen. For me, it was an adventure!

When I arrived at Marina's house, she asked me what I wanted her to buy for me. I asked for Coca-Cola. We walked together to the store, but when I saw a policeman, I froze in my tracks.

"Izidor, what's wrong?" she asked.

"There is a policeman over there and I am afraid of the police."

"Why are you afraid?"

"Because I heard that the police beat you and will cut off your hands if you steal."

"It's not true. This policeman is very nice."

I continued walking, but because I could not control my balance, I kept falling on my knees so we returned back home. Marina said she would get the Coca-Cola herself and I could stay home until she returned. Once she locked the door, I sat on the bed, trembling and scared to death because I was alone for the first time in my life.

Suddenly, someone knocked at the door. I was even more scared now. I could hear my heart pounding. That's how scared I was of being home alone for the first time. I hoped whoever was knocking wouldn't break in and kill me! Rather then opening the door, I sat on the bed, shaking and scared as could be. After three knocks, whoever it was went away.

When Marina returned, I had told her that someone knocked at the door.

"Did you answer it?"

"No, I just sat still."

"Oh, it was probably one of my friends who lives nearby."

That night, I asked Marina if I could call Melinda and Shawnee's house. She said I could call them anytime I wanted so I called to see how they were doing, and I told them I would write to them once I got to America. That night, Anca came over to see us. Marina told Anca that I had called Melinda and Shawnee's place a few times. Anca told me to call them again and tell them I was going to America the next day. After I had hung up with them, Anca told me not to call them again.

"Anca, are we really going to go to America tomorrow?"

"No, it was the only way for them not to speak with you," she said.

For some reason, Anca was filled with hatred and seemed not to like Chiprain and me. All she wanted was to get us to America and get her money from our new parents. She seemed so different from her husband. Today, I wonder if they are still together.

A few days later Anca called Marina's house and told her that I needed to be ready when she picked me up. Chiprain and I were finally going to America. That night, Marina's son Marius cooked dinner for all of us while his wife finished paperwork that had to be done in order for us to leave Romania.

Chiprain was really bad that night. I think the excitement was too much for him. When Marius left the kitchen to get something, he picked up a lighter and started setting things on fire. I stopped him. Everything he put his hands on, he ended up breaking. Many times Anca lost her temper with him. When she took a break from doing our paperwork to help Marius with dinner, she caught him typing on the paperwork that she had been trying to get done for weeks. Furious, she screamed at him and told him to go to bed and not to come out until tomorrow, but Marius told her the boy needed to eat before he went to bed.

While dinner cooked, I offered to help Marius. Within a few minutes, Chiprian found another lighter and started playing with it. I went and told Marius that he was playing with a lighter again. He returned to the kitchen and saw Chiprian trying to burn their tablecloth. When Marius saw this, he took the lighter away from him and hit him on the back with his hand. He told Chiprain to sit down and not to touch anything.

When Marius hit Chiprian, I really couldn't blame him because the boy never listened until he finally hit him. When Anca hit him, he never listened to her, but when Marius hit him for the first time, he listened. I think Chiprian knew Marius was angry with him and that he had gone too far on disobeying him. Marius liked Chiprian and Chiprian always listened to Marius until that night. Perhaps it was the different surroundings; perhaps it was the excitement of going to America. Perhaps it is just normal behavior for an FAS kid.

After dinner, Chiprian took a bath and was put to bed. He wouldn't fall asleep, so Anca had her dog bark at him, trying to scare him, but he wasn't scared of the dog, which made Anca even more angry. Marius went into the room and asked Chiprian if he would go to sleep for him. After he fell asleep, I took my bath and got ready for bed. When I came out of the bathroom, I heard Marius crying. I went into the living room to see if he was okay. Anca asked him why he was crying. Marius said he felt really guilty for hitting Chiprain. Anca told Marius that he got what he deserved and to stop feeling bad about it.

In the morning, we all woke up early to get ready to go to the airport, but we had to wait for someone who would come with us. I felt nervous just waiting around so I cleaned the house. I dusted all the furniture, vacuumed the carpet, and washed the windows. Finally, the person arrived and we headed directly to the airport and our flight to New York City where we would stay overnight.

During the flight Chiprian was hyper and could not sit still. In order to keep him calm, Anca drugged him and he fell asleep in his seat. When we landed in New York, it was already late at night, but I sat in awe at the blanket of lights that lay below on our approach.

When we arrived at our hotel Marius had a hard time getting a key for our room. He had to talk for a long time to the manager. Meanwhile, I was so tired I slid to the floor in the hallway, asleep, but Chiprain had to be kept with Anca and Marius. An hour later, when he finally got the key to our room, he had to pick me up and carry me to my bed. I was too exhausted to move.

---

## Chapter Seventeen

### Welcome to the United States of America

The next day, October 29, 1991, although still exhausted, we had to be up before dawn. Our *America West* flight was scheduled to leave at seven o'clock and we had to be at the airport early in case there were any paperwork delays. *No delays!* At the appointed hour we were on our way to California, and by two that afternoon, we landed in the sunshine at the San Diego Airport.

We were the last ones to get off the plane. As Chiprian and I walked from the plane, we heard crowds of people clapping and shouting, welcoming us to the United States of America and joining us with our new families. When we came into the terminal, all my eyes could take in was a sea of faces, some weeping, all smiling, and in the middle of that crowd, was my new mother, Marlys, kneeling, with her welcoming arms outstretched, waiting to embrace me.

I hugged my mother and she took me inside a special room to meet the rest of my family, but all I wanted to do was look around, to see what America looked like. Suddenly, I saw my friends from the hospital, Izabela and Calin. They were here! Here, in this America, too. Then I saw my American friends, Anna, Johnny, Ann and Debbie, the people who had made my journey to America possible. I was so glad to see everyone, especially Johnny and the two from my hospital family; I never thought I would see them again in my life.

I went to Izabela and hugged her. "You have a new wheelchair," I observed.

She nodded and smiled.

I put my hand on Izabela's hand and asked her, "Who is your mother?"

"My mother is your mother, Izidor," said Izabela.

I didn't like the sound of that. Although Izabela and I had been fast childhood friends, we had not been on good terms when she left the hospital. Someone had told me that she had gotten an operation so she could walk again. I was so happy for her and went to her bed, lifting the covers so I could see if it was true. She screamed at me to stop looking at her bare legs, then reported me to a nanny that I had tried to do something nasty, which was the farthest thing from my mind, and I was punished. That ended our close friendship.

No, I didn't like her answer, so I asked her again. More clearly. Maybe I had just misunderstood her. "Izabela, who is your mother here in America?"

Her response was the same as the first, so I asked her one last time. She wasn't making any sense to me. Why would she want to live with me when she had made such bad accusations about me and knew I no longer trusted her?

"Izidor, you and I have the same mother." She pointed towards Marlys.

I finally got it! This would take some getting used to, but I decided that I'd have to forgive her. "So, you and I... now we are sister and brother?"

She nodded happily.

Poor Chiprian was sick when he got off the plane. He threw up and could hardly stand while we received many gifts from people who had been waiting a long time for our arrival. They were members of a Romanian church and friends of my new parents. I especially liked a large brown teddy bear I could hug.

Our reunion was wonderful, to see the children who had gotten out of Romania two years ago, familiar faces in a strange new land. Then they had a surprise for me. In our language, my friends thanked me for my continued pushing and prodding at Johnny to rescue more friends, me included. The presentation ended with a special song they wrote in my honor. I felt very proud. But there still were more children to rescue so I didn't plan on ending my campaign to get Johnny to go back again.

After I got to see the whole airport, I asked Marlys this question. "Mom, can you show me my new room now?"

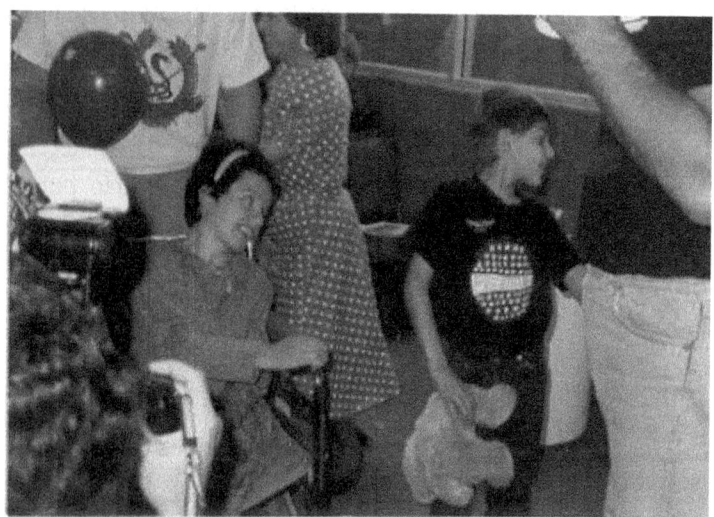

Everyone laughed, thinking it was funny because I thought the airport was my home.

"This is only the airport, Izidor, not our home," said Marlys.

Soon we went outside to the car. I couldn't believe how many cars I saw in the parking lot. Never in my life, not even in Romania, had I ever seen so many cars! My new family owned a very big car called a *Ford Aerostar*. It was new and big enough to hold all seven of us. My new dad, Daniel Ruckel, drove us home. When we got to the house, there was a big sign on the door that said, "Welcome home, Izidor." It made me feel very good inside.

I explored the ranch-style house, from top to bottom, looking into each room, opening every door, finding closets and storage places filled with supplies, clothing, shoes and other possessions. Everywhere, there were treasures. *So this is what an American home looks like!* I thought. I even had my own bedroom! My oldest sister, Jennifer Ruckel, gave it to me, even before I came to America. I also learned I now had four sisters; Jennifer, Robin, Cari, and Izabela.

The first day, Ann and her family came over to visit at our house. The second day, Chiprian and his family came over for a BBQ dinner. My dad, Daniel, had to go and get something from the store. Chiprian and I went with him; we were curious about stores in America. I could not believe how big the American stores were compared to the Romanian shops. The shelves were filled with bright colored products, most of which I had never before seen.

On the third day, I had my first bad day in America. It was my mother's birthday and she planned to take us out to lunch. When we got into the car, she asked me to put on my seat belt. I didn't understand her the first, second, or the third time, until she showed me what she wanted me to do. I understood it then: put on the seat belt. I didn't have to wear a seat belt in Romania, so I refused to put it on. My mother insisted all the way to McDonald's.

I was so angry because she wanted to trap me inside that seat belt, just like the nannies did with the straightjackets on the wild kids. I wasn't going to try to escape; America is where I'd longed to live since watching those *Dallas* television programs.

Because I got so angry, she said we would have to go back home. As we walked to the car, I angrily threw down a pack of gum and the fanny pack my sister, Jennifer, had given to me. I was about to throw away money as well, when I realized it was American money. I suppose I was not so crazy that I forgot the value of money! I put the money back into my pocket and watched as an old man picked up the gum. We argued and fought until we got home.

"Izidor, listen to Mom," Izabela told me in our language.

I told Izabela to shut up, but the look of horror on her face made it seem like I had said something completely awful, and she began to cry. *Up to her old tricks!* I told myself. *Not this time!*

Then she started calling me names and I returned the "favor," all in Romanian. My mother and sisters did not understand what we were saying, but they sensed we were using foul language so they all started to cry, too. *What was this?* I asked myself. *At the hospital, with the other kids, I was always the boss. At the hospital, four crying women was nothing!*

Mom tried to hug me to let me know that everything was going to be okay, but I knew so little English and she knew no Romanian that I didn't understand. When she got too close, I raised my left hand as if I was going to hit her, but she kept on walking towards me. When she got close to me, I knew that would be wrong and I lowered my hand. She tried to hug me, but I refused to accept it.

Jennifer, Robin and Cari thought Mom would send me back to the hospital. In my heart I thought she would say the words. "Izidor, you are going back to the hospital." Like a miracle, she never said anything like that. Instead, she called one of her friends who spoke Romanian. She wanted him to explain to me that I needed to wear the seat belt anywhere we went.

When he arrived, I refused to speak with him. I was so mixed up and afraid. Even in the chaos of the hospital I was often the one in control and could usually figure out what to do next. But here? In America? I felt stupid.

That night, my mom invited a couple over for dinner. When my father came home from work she told him everything that had happened that day. Soon the couple arrived. Viorel and Adina had two children of their own, adopted from Romania, as well. Whenever they came to see Izabela and me, they always brought gifts and Romanian music. Viorel also explained some of the rules of the United States that we had to follow.

"If you don't wear a seat belt, then your parents could go to prison," he explained. After he told me that, I understood and always wore the seat belt everywhere I went.

A few weeks later, my parents took Izabela and me to the Romanian church in Orange County. My parents wanted us to meet some friends who spoke the Romanian language so we wouldn't forget it. The church was so packed when we got there that people stood outside to listen. After the service we stayed and talked with people, although I didn't know anyone except Viorel and Adina. Before we left, Izabela and I received Romanian music from a man we didn't know.

We didn't return home till nightfall. Sometimes my whole family went to the Romanian church, although my American sisters didn't understand what the preacher was saying, because it was all in the Romanian language.

**THE RUCKEL FAMILY**
back row: DANNY, MARLYS, JENNIFER
front row: ROBIN, IZIDOR, IZABELA, CARI

## Chapter Eighteen

### One year later

On Sunday Izabela and Mom went to the Romanian church. I decided to stay home with Dad. I was already asleep when they got home, but in the morning, Izabela told me that Adina had died.

I didn't believe her. "Izabela, she is not dead." When I walked downstairs, I saw Mom crying and she confirmed the news. I was heartbroken. I just couldn't believe that my close friend was gone.

At the funeral, when I saw Adina's body lying in the casket, I broke into tears, knowing how much I was going to miss her. She had died because she had problems with her kidneys. A few weeks later, Viorel and the children moved to a different state. That was the last time we ever saw them.

We continued going to the Romanian church, and we always met new people. When Adriana and Vasile invited us over for dinner, they cooked Romanian food -- one of the best Romanian cakes I ever tasted and the basics, cornmeal mush and cabbage roll.

That night, the couple taught Izabela and me about God and Jesus Christ. How Jesus had died on the cross for me to live today. I recalled the night in Romania when I'd first seen the big statue and was told it was "Mr. Jesus Christ." It took me a while before I could understand anything about the Bible, but the more I didn't understand, the more questions I asked Adriana.

"Why did Jesus Christ die for me?" I asked.

"Jesus Christ died for you because he loves you very much," she replied. "Izidor, did you know that God helped you come to America?"

By the time we left their house, I was excited to learn how God had loved me while I was in the hospital and had helped me come to America without me even knowing about it. This was big news for me; I always knew what was going on at the hospital!

~~~~~~~~~~~~~~~~~~~~~~~~~~~~~~~

## Chapter Nineteen

### Going to school

Most of my new friends went to public school. Since they went to public school, I wanted to go there as well. My parents really wanted to home-school me like Jennifer, Robin and Cari. Only Izabela went to public school, and that was because she needed special education and training. After begging them for weeks and weeks, they finally decided to give it a chance.

The first time I went to the school, I went only to meet all my classmates and my teachers, but within a few weeks, I began my studies. On my first day, Mom walked with me to the school so I could get the idea of getting to school on my own. As we were crossing a street, I stopped right in the middle to wave to a police officer, but my mouth dropped open when I saw a woman in the police car. I looked at my mom in astonishment.

"Women can't be police," I said. "They're supposed to be at home cleaning the house."

My mother chuckled at my judgment. "Here in America, women can be police if they want to be."

This news was another revelation!

In school I attended the ESL (English Second Language) class. This is how I was supposed to learn to read: the teacher read a book to me first and I repeated what she read. To them, that was teaching me how to read. Within a few weeks, I went home with the book and read it to my mom.

"Izidor, I bet you can read that book behind your back," said my mother.

I put the book behind my back and, sure enough, I could read it without even looking at the pages. Mom's suspicions were correct. I had memorized the words!

The next day, my mom went to the school, angry, asking questions about my ability to read and my education. The principal told my parents that, at age eleven, I was too old to learn anything. Of course, that is nonsense. I was home-schooled after that, and am now attending Mt. San Jacinto Community College under a full scholarship.

During that summer, while everyone else was out of school, my family took the time to teach me my ABC's and the nouns. They taught me to actually read from trying, not from someone reading to me first. After I read my first book: "The Pig Sat on the Mud," I was so excited when I finished it I had to tell my neighbor. After I read it to her, she was so excited for me that she gave me five dollars!

What a deal! I thought. I wanted to read my book for all the neighbors. My parents said that I could, but I shouldn't expect to get paid each time. The five dollars had been a special gift.

When school started in the Fall, I was home-schooled with Jennifer, Robin and Cari. The first thing I learned was history, about the Indians and how they helped the Pilgrims grow crops and celebrate Thanksgiving in peace. The next summer, my sisters joined a softball league. My dad coached Robin and Cari's team. Jennifer played with a different league. Izabela couldn't play because of her disability, but she was always there cheering on everyone.

I didn't know how to play any sports yet, but every time the girls had their games, I ended up playing catch with some of the kids who were just there to watch, too.

## Chapter Twenty

### More children come to America

One afternoon, the phone rang and Mom answered as my sisters and I watched television in the living room. After a few minutes, I noticed she was on the phone for quite a while. In my mind, I thought she was just visiting with one of her friends. The next thing I knew she ran upstairs, crying. We all asked her if anything was wrong?

"No, everything is fine," she said in a tremulous voice.

But everything didn't sound fine to us. Finally, Mom came back downstairs, crying more than ever. Now we knew something was terribly wrong and went to her to find out.

"Mom, what's wrong? Tell us," said Jennifer.

"That was John Upton on the phone," she said, "calling from Romania. He's coming back with eleven children."

"Is John bringing Christina, Anita and Jannia with him?" I asked.

"Christina and Jannia are coming, but Anita's parents took her home with them and she is not coming."

I was sad to hear about that. Before John had gone to Romania he asked me whom I wanted him to bring home with him to America? I gave him a list. "Bring Anita, Jannia and Christina to America." Christina and Jannia were coming, but Anita remained behind. I knew John could do nothing without the permission of Anita's parents. They made the decision to take her home. For what purpose, I wondered, since they never wanted her before?

Two days later, we dressed in our best clothes and went to meet the children and John at the San Diego Embassy Suites Hotel. When we arrived, there were already more than two-hundred people waiting to celebrate. John and the kids arrived at eight o'clock. Izabela, Anna, Calin, Chiprian and I were there to meet the kids.

It was a great reunion. We all came from the same hospital so we knew all the kids John brought this time. *ABC News 20/20* went to Romania with John to do a follow-up story on his mission of getting children out of the hospital. Before the kids entered the hotel, the camera crew lined us up where they could see us as they entered. As they arrived, Christina, Jannia, and Elena ran to hug Izabela and me, the first people they recognized. Calin and Roxana, the Romanian translators, were tired when they came into the hotel. Everyone was so excited to see the eleven children who had just come from the Romanian hospital. Everywhere I looked, there was someone asking what one child was saying? I ended up being the translator for the night, and that suited me fine.

**New Arrivals in America**

Toward the end of the night, someone called my name as I translated. *ABC News 20/20* wanted to ask me some questions about my friends who had just arrived from the hospital. The press had never interviewed me before, so I didn't quite know how to respond to their questions. My parents sat right across from me, helping me to answer, but rather then letting them help me, I needed to feel in control again, especially around all the Romanian children who had always respected me, so I told them to SHUT UP! Everyone laughed, although I doubt my parents thought it funny. It was rude. The person who asked me questions was Janice Tomlin, producer for *ABC News 20/20*.

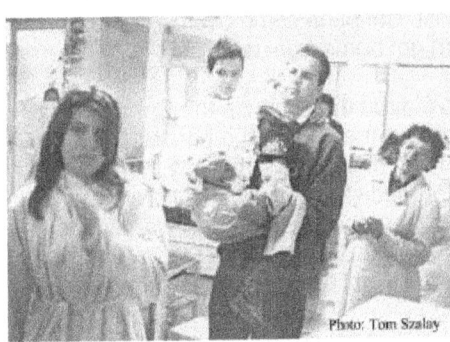

ELENA IN JOHNNY'S ARMS

All the children needed a family to stay with for one week until they went to Virginia. My parents took in Elena and Anna Mica (Little Anna). Izabela and I wanted Jannia to stay with us, but John didn't want her to stay with us for some reason.

I didn't mind Elena staying with us, but Anna Mica was too much of a troublemaker. My parents wouldn't listen and she came to our home.

That night, we left the hotel around midnight. When we got home, Anna already began her habit of spitting. Since she was a little child, she loved spitting on people and on things. My parents had a hard time getting Anna to sleep. I had to be a bit aggressive in order for Anna to listen to my parents. Sure enough, she listened when I stepped in and scolded in Romanian.

Elena was like an angel; obedient and listened to my parents very well. The next morning when I got up, Elena and Anna Mica were already awake. My mom gave Anna a bottle of liquid soap and a bubble blower but, rather then blow bubbles, Anna drank it, and immediately started burping bubbles out of her mouth. My mom got scared when she saw bubbles coming out of Anna's mouth, but I told her that was normal for her to do.

Since Anna and Elena didn't have clothes to wear, my sisters gave them each a dress of their own. Anna loved wearing dresses, but she had one dress she wanted to wear every day. My parents tried giving her a new dress so the other one could be washed, but because Anna couldn't get her way, she lifted her dress and went to the bathroom right on the living room carpet. After what she did, I wanted to smack her, but my parents, always calm about everything, told me that we needed to just show love. I would have done that *after* I'd smacked her!

Within a few weeks, all the girls who stayed with families in California went to Virginia to their new families. I kept in touch with Jannia and Christina the most. Christina came over to our house every morning until her mom got home from work.

Soon *ABC News 20/20* aired the show on the Romanian orphans and how Americans had tried to get the parents they found, after many false starts, to sign papers to allow their child to come to the United States for medical treatment. Children who were left behind had broken hearts because they all wanted to come to America. The title of the story was *"Take Me to America,"* produced by my friends, Janice Tomlin and reporter Tom Jarriel.

The story seemed to be more focused on one little boy who was more heartbroken than anyone in that hospital. He was my friend; his name was Marin. His parents could not be located anywhere. Johnny hired people to find them. They even tried to find his grandfather. Nothing but false leads. Therefore, Johnny was not able to bring him to America. Poor Marin could not understand the reason why he had to stay behind.

I called John after I saw the program. "John, you cannot leave Marin there. When will you go back for him? You *must* go back to get more of my friends from the hospital."

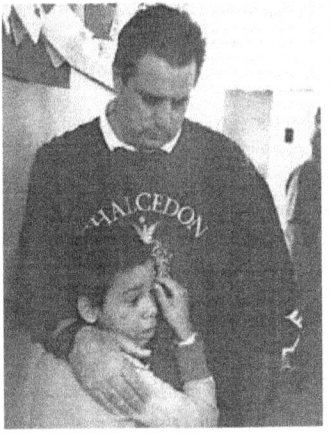

MARIN AND JOHN

A month later John returned to Romania for more children, and this time Marin got to come to America. It was such a fast rescue that Marin didn't yet have an American family of his own. At first, he stayed with John, and for two weeks he stayed with us until a family was found for him. We all prayed that God would find a good family for him. Within a few weeks, a family was found in Sacramento.

## Chapter Twenty-one

### Shriners Hospital

When I came to the United States I kept doctor's appointments to find out about my sick legs. At the same time doctors tried to figure out what had caused my disability that caused me to walk with a limp on my right leg. No one seemed able to solve the mystery so one of our doctors recommended that we go to the *Shriners Hospital for Disabled Children* in Los Angeles.

The doctor I saw at Shriners Hospital was Dr. Bernsten, who would discover why I had a disability and why it was hard for some doctors to find; at first, not even Dr. Bernsten was able to find out the cause. I had to return six months later to run more tests and X-rays. Then the doctor discovered I'd had Polio in my babyhood. The reason it was hard to detect was because Polio is not a common disease anymore since Dr. Salk created the polio vaccine in 1955.

He told me that large outbreaks of Polio occurred throughout Europe and the United States in the 1800's. In 1916, Polio killed over 6,000 people and 27,000 people were paralyzed. Today Polio is not common because every child at an early age receives vaccine against it.

Upon consultation, Dr. Bernsten decided to amputate my right leg. I would not agree to it. I did not come to America to have my leg cut off! I told the doctor to search for an alternative and went back home. I had to return within six months and I heard good news! They did come up with an alternate plan.

On January 11, 1995, I went to Shriners hospital for an operation on my left leg. They hoped to make my left leg grow slower, so my right leg could catch up. The operation they performed is called an *epiphysiodesis of the distal femur and proximal fibula and tibia*. The name alone was enough to frighten me to death!

On the day of surgery I was so scared. My family came to see me about twenty minutes before I was drugged and taken to surgery. As I took the medication to put me to sleep, I cried and cried, because it was the first operation of my life. John told me I would have an operation in America and, sure enough, here I was.

When I woke up seven hours later, everyone in my family was gone expect my mom. She stayed overnight with me. Shortly after I awaken I got sick from the medications, which was normal if you drank it.

In most cases, when you have an operation, you get a shot to put you to sleep. In my case, I was scared of the needles after my Romanian hospital experiences where I'd seen so many children die from dirty ones, so I was allowed to drink the liquid medication instead. On my second day in the hospital I was supposed to be released, but Dr. Bernsten decided to keep me another day to make sure everything turned out as planned in the operating room.

## Chapter Twenty-two

### The Ruckle Athletes

Every summer Cari and I always met new friends who had either moved into the neighborhood or visited for the summer with grandparents or a divorced parent. We all played baseball and that's how I made new friends, by playing a sport that was well known to everyone. Most of the time, kids from the whole neighborhood joined the game. If my team began losing, then I began coaching, because I couldn't stand losing any game I played. In American I had to do more than survive; I had to win!

Two of the guys who played baseball with us went to Mt. Carmel High School in San Diego. Both of them played on the school's baseball team. Eric Chivez and Carl were our neighbors. Jennifer and I went to a few of their practice games to see them play.

One night after I came home from their practice, I got a telephone call from Carl, and he wanted to know if I'd like to be a batboy for their baseball team. I told him I'd be honored. Every game they played, whether at home or away, I was there. I went everywhere with the team because I was actually part of the team.

One of the main things I noticed about Eric Chivez was that he was a very good hitter. Almost every time at bat he hit a home run. When their games were at home, my sister Jennifer drove me to their games and, when they were away, I went on the bus with the rest of the team.

In the summer of 1995, the Mt. Carmel baseball team made it to the C.I.F. (*California Individual Finals*) Championship held at the *San Diego Padres Stadium*. The *Mt. Carmel Sundevils* faced the *Ranch Bernardo Broncos* for the championship. It was an awesome game because the Mt. Carmel team won the game by eleven points; the score was 11 to 0. The reason they won? Our team had a really good pitcher, and some really good hitters.

The following year I was asked again to be the batboy, but this time I was unable to accept because my family was in the process of moving to Temecula, several hours away. Half the team graduated that year, among them, Eric Chivez. He accepted an offer to play in the minor league for the Oakland A's. Within a few years he stepped up to the Oakland major league team.

My family and I traveled all the way to Arizona for spring training, to see Eric play. I went to the front row to speak to him and he signed his baseball bat for me and gave to me. I still have it. He signed a contract for over a million dollars and, with the money he helped out his family and bought them each a gift. Carl moved on with his life and I never saw him after the second year of baseball.

## Temecula Valley

November 20, 1996, we moved to Temecula because we needed a bigger house since there were seven of us. We found a very nice house with four bedrooms, four bathrooms, two living rooms and a huge kitchen. I still had my own bedroom, but a larger one.

Jennifer and Robin stayed inside the house most of the time, while Cari and I were outside playing sports with new friends that we made. A few weeks later, I joined a bowling league. My games were every Saturday morning from 9:00 a.m. to 11:00 a.m.

At the same time, my parents wanted me to start going to public school because every time I didn't get a good grade in math and history in home-school, I'd end up flustered, losing my temper and acting out. I expected to get a good grade like all the other kids my age. Just as in my team competition, I didn't like to lose in my studies either. On December 5, I entered the *Temecula Valley High School.* I already knew quite a few people at the school, friends from the neighborhood and from the bowling team so that made the start easier.

My first semester, I worked as hard as I could to get a good grade in all my classes. All homework was typed, hoping I could get extra credit for neatness. Most of the time, I did get that extra credit because it made it easier for teachers to read my reports. My handwriting lacks legibility! I only had one class I hated -- biology. My GPA (Grade Point Average) for the semester was 2.8, which satisfied me. My friend Marco got a 3.0 GPA and Nick Bell got the same grade as me, but I still hated biology!

On September 17, 1996, I had another operation on my left leg at Shriners hospital. This time the operation was to correct the bones that were overgrown and twisted. The operation is called, "triple Arthrodesis" -- another scary name.

This time I was given a walking cast. Within a few days I returned to school. My cast didn't last long because I got it wet by walking in the rain and letting the water run inside. It turned to mush. I had to go back to Shriners to get a new cast, and Dr. Bernsten said to take care of this one because I had to wear it for six months before it could come off. In the meantime I continued returning to Shriners for checkups and x-rays until the cast was removed and I could walk again, only better.

May of 1997, Marco, my next door neighbor, and I decided to try out for the *Temecula Swim Team*. When we went to try out, I wasn't worried if Marco would make the team or not. I knew he probably would, but I wasn't so sure I was going to make the team. Sandy, coach of the swim team, asked us to swim freestyle, backstroke, butterfly and breaststroke. I had no idea how to do any of those strokes, but all Coach Sandy was looking for was to see if we were able to swim a full length of the pool. I barely made the length, so now I had to wait for the coach's call to see if we made the team.

Two days later, after school, Marco and I got our answer -- we both made the swim team and we celebrated the good news. The next day, Marco and I went to our first practice and we were put with the beginners until we improved.

Just swimming for an hour made me tired, but I continued to swim on the team, no matter how hard it was. The only thing I couldn't do that most other kids could, was use my legs. I never used my legs because it was harder for me to swim if I tried to kick. Not using my legs slowed me down and I was not able to swim as fast as the other swimmers.

Because swimming and bowling started at the same time, I had to finish my bowling leagues on Thursdays instead of Saturdays. Our first swim meet was in March against Yucca Valley, one of the best teams in the league. I swam in three events, backstroke, freestyle and butterfly. Although the butterfly was not my best stroke, Coach Sandy always had me do the butterfly. We lost our first meet, but better luck next time.

On Monday when we went to practice, Coach Sandy gave us our ribbons from the Saturday competition. I got two ribbons that day. I was surprised that I even got one because I had come in last place in all the events. I asked Coach Sandy why I got the ribbons if I came in last place.

"You got those ribbons because most of the people you swam against got disqualified and that brought you to second and third place," Coach Sandy explained.

We had to practice five days a week and I got stronger. My shoulders, back and arms showed my strength. On Saturdays, we competed from 9:00 a.m. to 1:00 p.m. A few weeks after our competitions began, I was moved up a level. There were three levels, all together. One was the beginner's group, second was the middle group advanced, and third was the high school group.

When I first joined the swim team, I practiced from 3:30 p.m. to 4:40 p.m., but when I got moved to the next level, I had to swim from 4:30 p.m. to 5:30 p.m. The workout was much harder than the beginner's group. Soon after, Marco had to leave the team because soccer tryouts were coming up and he couldn't do both. I chose to stay on the team.

Every swim competition that I entered, my family always came to support me. There were many times when I came in last place, but here's the funny thing -- every team we swam against always cheered our team to finish our laps. There were times when I wanted to stop right in the middle of the pool because I felt so tired, but when you have your team and the other team cheering you on, it gives you more power to finish. How could I give up?

A few months later, my sisters Robin and Cari decided to join the swim team too, but they had to start in the middle group. June 21 was our last competition for the year. Our team came in third place in the league. Before everyone could leave, Robin, Cari and I asked the team if they'd like to get something for the coaches? Everyone put their money together and gave it to my mom to purchase the coaches' surprise gifts.

## Ceremony Awards

On July 21 we had our swim team awards ceremony. Everyone got a trophy for participating on the team. Some people got more then this basic award. I was surprised and honored to receive the *Coach's Award* for Best Improved Team Member. I couldn't stop grinning when everyone clapped and whistled. After Coach Sandy finished the awards, Robin and I walked on stage and presented the gifts from the team. The coaches were very pleased to receive a tribute from the whole team. Afterward we had a party, a *swim party* with friends and family.

Robin, Cari and I swam at the C.I.F. Championship, too. I came in last place for all of my events so I didn't qualify, but that was okay with me because the three of us signed up for swimming in the California State Games instead. The State Games was more like the Junior Olympics where you could play just about any sport with kids from all over the United States. I loved the idea of making more new friends in America. These games were held in Orange County so, rather than commuting daily, we stayed at a hotel.

At the evening Opening Ceremony, held at a university football stadium, all you could see was a forest of standing fans, cheering us as we walked onto the field. There were about ten local news cameras and reporters. They estimated that over 6,000 people watched more than 4,000 athletes gathered here to play a sport. I looked around me and the field was packed with competitors. I was right in the middle of where I wanted to be -- competing!

As the ceremony began, the torch was lit and we sang the *National Anthem* and *"God Bless America."* We even had professional athletes who had played their sports in the Olympics years ago. The ceremony lasted three hours. I was excited because I felt like I was actually on a real Olympic team.

In the morning, we were up by five o'clock and went to get checked in for our events. Weighing my competition and odds of winning, I asked the lady how many people were going to swim the backstroke?

"Only two people," she said.

Now I knew I had a chance to win a gold medal. In all the other events, I swam against twelve guys. My events were backstroke, freestyle and butterfly. I figured I'd come in last in the butterfly because I always did, every time I swam that event. I even told Coach Sandy that I didn't want to do the butterfly anymore, but she would not take me out because she wanted me to get used to doing it.

"The more you do your butterfly, the better you will get at it," she said.

I accepted her answer and continued to swim butterfly in all my events.

Competition started early and we swam four events that day. Cari and Robin swam very well. In backstroke, I came in second place; in butterfly, I came in last place; in the freestyle, I came in last. It was still worth coming in last place because to me it was an honor to compete in the California State Games.

Toward the end of my event, Cari told me I'd won three medals. I didn't believe her and had to check it out for myself. Sure enough, it was true: Two bronzes and one silver medal!

I didn't feel like I had really earned those three medals. For a minute, I thought Coach Sandy was giving me some extra attention because of my leg disability so I asked her. She got angry that I would even think something like that.

"I treat you as I treat all the other swimmers and you do not have a disability," Coach Sandy proclaimed.

I believed her when she told me that.

## Chapter Twenty-three

### High School

For the first time, the *Temecula Valley High* was starting their own swim team. I made the team in my sophomore year. Daily practice ran an hour and a half, and started right after school at 2:30 p.m. The boys' coach was Mike, and the girls' coach was Jennifer.

When I first joined the *Temecula Valley High School Swim Team*, I expected a rough workout but, to tell you the truth, it wasn't nearly as demanding as Coach Sandy's workouts. She had prepared me well.

In April, we had our first competition, which was away. I loved to swim for the high school because one of the perks was you got out of school an hour earlier when our meets were away. When the meets were at home, we still had to stay in school until the last bell. Anyone who did not show up the day before the meet didn't get to swim in the competition.

We had over 100 girls on the Women's team and about 50 guys on the Men's team. There weren't enough guys on the team so, every time we competed, all the guys had to swim. In a way, I was glad that we didn't have enough guys because not all the guys would have been able to swim in the away meets. I didn't want to be one of those guys left behind, but in my case that never happened.

I loved swimming and I loved to teach swimming, but for some reason, I was always cold in the water when I swam for the high school team. I made excuses to go to the bathroom, but I really took a hot shower every time I got out of the pool. It wasn't long before the coach caught up with me. At one of our practices, he came into the bathroom to check on me since I took so long, but he didn't yell.

"I was just making sure you didn't fall in the toilet or any thing." Then he walked out.

Most of the time when I swam at practice, I picked someone next to my lane and challenged him to see if I could beat him, without that person knowing I was swimming against him. My lifelong competitive spirit served me well in swimming races.

On July 20 we had our high school Awards Banquet for the swim team. One of the awards I received was the funny "Wally Whiner" Award, given "because I always whined and asked to go to the bathroom." The second award I received was for participation on the team. Everyone got a funny award and a participation award. There were only seven people to receive a "serious" trophy out of the 150 swimmers on our teams. I was one of those people to receive a trophy. It was a most unexpected honor.

Most of the kids went back to Coach Sandy's team because the high school's swim team was over for the year. I never went back because my parents would not allow me to continue swimming when my school grades began to fall. That was the last time I ever swam on a swim team.

Although I was taken off the swim team, my grades continued to fall and I began fighting with my parents. It was a sad time for us all. Three years after I arrived in the United States, I became homesick and sometimes I got very confused in my mind because I had wanted to go back to Romania. My parents asked if there was anything they could do to help me, but instead of letting my parents help me, I rejected them.

As weeks, months and years went by, I became more and more mixed up and I took it out on my parents and sisters. As my anger grew worse, I began using foul language towards my family. Hearing me use foul language was a shock to my parents because they had never heard me use it. If they didn't hear me use it, one of my friends would tell my parents.

I was so mixed up that every time I got into an argument with my family, I always wanted them to say: "Izidor, we wish we had never adopted you and we are going to send you back to the hospital."

But no one ever said that.

When I got sent to my room, I blasted my Romanian music or I'd bang on the door as hard as I could with anything I could find -- a book, my shoe, my fist. One night, I came home from work at Carl's Jr. and I threw my backpack in the garage, then went to see one of my friends. When I returned, I got into an argument with Jennifer. I told her to shut up. My mom heard me say that. She told me that if I couldn't be nice to people, then I needed to go to my room. As she talked to me, I walked away and ignored her. My dad came into the room and said that I needed to look at my mom when she talked to me.

That's when I lost my temper with my whole family and told my dad, "Fuck you!" I tried walking out, but my dad grabbed me by the shirt and told me to stay inside the house. I reared back and hit my father. Rather than hitting me back, he pinned me down to the ground and called the police. As he pinned me and I tried to twist away, I kept screaming, *"I hate you, you fucking bastard!"*

When the police arrived, I was handcuffed and taken out to the squad car while the officers talked with my parents.

I told the police I wanted to be put in foster care. "Living with those people is like living in hell."

A few days later, I went to work and I closed that night. When I got off work, I walked home and it was two o'clock in the morning when I got there. I knocked on the door and there was no response. I tried knocking over and over and nobody answered the door. Finally, I got it -- I knew I was kicked out of the house.

That night, I slept at Marco's house. In the morning, I went to see if anyone was home. My mom opened the door and I asked if I could come in.

"You'll have to wait until Dad gets home," she said. "In the meantime, I put all of your things in the garage."

I went to look in the garage and, sure enough, found all my things sitting there. I asked Mom if I could get ready for work, but she said no. I turned to leave and she slammed the door behind me. That's when I spun around and kicked the door as hard as I could.

The door instantly opened. "If you break that door," she warned, "then you'll pay for it out of your check."

I gave my mother the dirtiest look I could make. "I don't care, you son of a bitch," I yelled.

"That's funny," she said, with tears in her eyes, "because girls can't be sons of bitches."

I had borrowed a friend's bike and went to work to pick up my check. I also went to get something to eat since I was three hours early for work. I was filled with anger and all I could think of was how much I hated my family. That night when I got off work, I went to a friend's house and stayed with Joanna for seven months. I didn't even want my parents to know where I was. At times, after fighting with them, I had thought about killing myself.

One day, I did go back to my parent's house to pick up some clothes. That's where my life began to change for the worse. Living with Joanna was fine. I never had any problems there, but that's where I started doing drugs, drinking alcohol, and going to strip clubs. Did Joanna care what I did? Why should she have cared when I wasn't even her son and I didn't care about her?

A few days later while I was at work, Robin and Jennifer came to speak with me. I took a ten-minute break and went outside to see what they wanted.

"I hear you're going to have your friends beat up Nick?" Jennifer accused.

"So what?" I grumbled, sneering. "Do you have a problem with that?"

She rose to her full height and looked me in the eye. "If you have your friends beat up Nick, I'll get all my friends to jump all your friends," Jennifer threatened.

"You came all this way to tell me that your sissy friend couldn't come here and stand up for himself?" I yelled. "Go home!" Then I went back into work.

Every day I felt bad for the wrongs I caused, but I could not show my family I was sorry for my mistakes. The reason I was going to have Nick beat up was because he was always the one to tell my parents everything I did. I remembered the threats of the house nannies and felt the sharp pain of their heavy oak broomstick so why not try threats and a beating on the one who snitched on me, just as I always took care of spies and snitches at the hospital?

Through Nick, my parents found out I was doing drugs and alcohol. I never wanted my parents to find out. He never got beat up, but I sure was angry with him. It was only later, after finding out the truth, that I discovered Nick had not been the one who told my parents about my drug use. Only in my mixed up mind, did I think it was so.

### June 20, 1998

On June 20 it was my 18$^{th}$ birthday and I had to work. My mom came to Joanna's house to see if I was home. Since I was not, Mom asked her to give me my gift. She also brought a decorated birthday cake for me. When Joanna told her she'd already made a cake, Mom took hers back home. That afternoon, Joanna came to my work with her cake and my family's gifts.

"Your mom came by and dropped these off for you," she said.

Suddenly, I just wanted to break down into tears because I knew my family was still there for me.

A few days later, I went to work a bit early to get my hair cut before I began my shift. The lady who cuts my hair knew my family very well.

"Hey, Izidor, did you hear what happened to your family?" Elena asked.

"I don't even care what happens to them," I said, still trying to act tough.

"Well, you ought to," she said, leaning into my face. "They got into a terrible car accident today. Robin is in a coma. Cari and your mom are in the hospital, too."

I got scared when she told me that. Ten minutes before I began my shift, I told my boss I couldn't work.

"Why can't you work today?"

"Because my family got into a car accident and I have to see if they're all right."

"But you need to work your shift," said my boss.

"I am not working. You can fire me if you want, but my family is more important than my work."

"All right, all right, calm down. We'll give you the day off, then."

Before I went to the hospital, I bought Robin, Cari and my mom three dozen roses and a get-well card. When I arrived I found out they had just left. I hurried to my parents' house, hoping they wouldn't slam the door in my face. I knocked at the door and my mom opened it. I stood there with tears in my eyes; Mom was safe! I took a deep breath and asked if I could come in.

"Sure, you can, Izidor," she replied. "Come in."

Remembering the bouquet, I laid it gently into her arms. "These are for you, Robin and Cari." While she admired the blooms, I whispered, "Mom, do you have a moment so I can speak with you?" She nodded and led the way to the kitchen.

After a quiet discussion with Mom, I believed there was a real chance that my problems with my family would finally be resolved. My mother and sisters forgave me. The only one I was scared to talk with was Dad. I should have known I didn't need to fear him. He spoke with me calmly and told me he would like for me to visit when I could.

"I know your sisters miss you and they would like to see you more often," he said.

My heart sang for joy! My family was willing to forgive me. That's when I started to change my life. I stopped doing drugs and drinking. I began going to church and youth group again, and I kept remembering Mr. Jesus Christ, who loved me and had died for my sins.

~~~~~~~~~~~~~~~~~~~~~~~~~~~~~~~~~

## Chapter Twenty-four

### San Jacinto

One of my friends, Kathy, who I worked with asked me if I wanted to move into her apartment in San Jacinto as roommates, along with her two kids, Daniel and Ruth, to help with the rent. I agreed because I needed to get out of where I was living.

Unfortunately, soon after I moved I lost my job and told her I had to leave, but she had an idea. Rather than kick me out, she asked me to watch her kids while she worked. That would make up for the rent, she said.

I agreed and baby-sat her kids five days a week for eight hours. Here I was, taking care of kids again. Sometimes I would have preferred to hang out with my friends, but I couldn't because

I'd given my word. Besides, Daniel was one of those kids you had to keep a close eye on. Mostly, it was easy duty. Although Daniel never listened to his mom, he listened to me... Or else!

This is how I handled things. By 6:30 p.m., the children had to come in for the night. They ate the dinner I cooked for them, then they showered. I had them get their clothes out, ready for school in the morning. After that, they did their homework. If they got done early, I let them watch television until 8:30 p.m. Bedtime. They both fell asleep quickly.

Once they were asleep, I cleaned the kitchen top to bottom and worked my way into the living room. After cleaning I watched television. Kathy got home from work at one o'clock. In the morning, Daniel and Ruth went to school and I looked for a job until class was out.

There was one thing I did not like: Kathy had another roommate, Chris, who was an abusive boyfriend. It bothered me very much, but I didn't know what I could do about it.

On New Year's Eve, 1998, I went to Knotts Berry Farm with a church youth group. We left around supper time to hear Christian bands and have some fun. When I got home at 4:00 a.m., one of my neighbors was standing on the balcony, smoking.

"Did you know Kathy is in the hospital?"

"No, I just got home. What happened?"

"Chris, that no-good-s.o.b. hit Kathy up side her head with the telephone."

"Is she okay now?"

"I guess, but she's in the hospital."

"Where are her kids?"

"I have them here with me," he said. "Kathy wanted me to tell you that she wanted you to watch them for her."

The neighbor carried Daniel into my apartment and laid him in his bed while Ruth walked with me. After the man left, I sat down with Ruth to find out what exactly did happen. It was an old story. Kathy and Chris got drunk and Chris started hitting her.

"My mom hit him back, and that's when Chris hit my mom with the telephone." Ruth began to cry.

"Where is Chris now?"

"The police took him to jail."

"It's about time that the police took him to jail," I muttered.

Ruth could not sleep and I wasn't going to insist; she was afraid. Later, I called the Hemet Hospital to find out if Kathy was there. No luck. I found her at the Moreno Valley Hospital. I called in sick for Kathy at her work. About 6:00 a.m. she walked in the door. What a surprise! Everyone made out like she was ready to die, but she just had a few marks on her face and a black eye.

A few days later, Kathy went back to work, but sometimes she didn't come home all night. I knew where she went. In the morning, I'd get Daniel and Ruth off to school. Ruth was no problem, but Daniel was a handful. Sometimes, watching him and putting up with his stuff, I felt like his father. That's when I'd say to myself, "Thank God, I don't have any kids."

When I began having bigger problems with Daniel, I told his mom I didn't want to watch him anymore. Kathy got upset with me and decided to put Ruth in charge. That's when I began seriously looking for work.

It took me six months to find a job. Soon after, I moved out with another roommate. After a year I left her, then moved with my third roommate, Jason. I worked with him at Carl's Jr., and he had asked me if I'd like to move in with him and his girl friend Katie to help with the rent?

My first night there I saw that the apartment was dirty and a mess. I told myself, *maybe they're not always like this.* I cleaned the place up, and an hour after they got home, it looked the same as before so I knew, for sure, that my new roommates were messy slobs. A few months later, something worse happened; my things began to disappear. First, it was my typewriter, then my computer, clothes, tapes, CDs and money. My roommates were thieves!

Later, I found out they sold my things to buy drugs. I couldn't understand how I was so blind. What was there for me to do when it was already too late? I stayed because I had nowhere else to go.

Within a few months, Jason got fired for not showing up three times in a row. He got more chances than he deserved. He also got in serious trouble for owing the wrong people, money. One guy even pulled a knife to cut him. What did I do? I helped Jason out and gave him a $200 loan, which was never returned, to pay off his debt.

Since I was able to work many extra hours and was short of free time, I gave Katie $200 to go pay off two of my loans. A few days later, I got a call from the loan company informing me that I was late on my payment. Late? Trusting Izidor got taken again! I explained how I'd given the money to a friend to repay the loan, but since she did not, I would make it up as soon as possible.

This time they would not get away with stealing from me. I told the pair, if they were not going to pay me back my money, then I was not going to pay rent for two months. This was a nightmare situation and I wasn't smart enough to leave. They'd both lost their jobs two months before. The phone was off, and the gas and electric got shut off because they didn't pay their bills. Jason never even bothered to look for a new job and Katie thought she didn't have to work.

By the end of the first month, they were already asking me to help them with the electric and rent. I was not going to give them another penny. I knew they would only use my money to buy drugs and beer. When I refused to help pay their bills, they told me to get out, but I was not willing to go until my last thirty days were up.

Well, that didn't work either because when I came home from work that night they'd locked me out of the apartment and I didn't have a key. What could I do at that point? I walked to the park and stayed there till morning, then I went to work.

Dana, my manager, offered to help me, but I refused. She had done a lot for me and had given me more chances than any other manager was likely to do. After I got off work, I went back to see if I could get in. I walked into the unlocked apartment and they came in soon after and told me to leave. Katie hit me with a towel. I grabbed it away and hit her back, telling her I was not her boyfriend.

They called the police on me, but the police told them they could not kick me out until they gave me my thirty day's notice.

"What if they lock me out again?"

"If they do, just call us and we'll come back and arrest them."

Katie was so angry with me that they left for the night. I was home alone so all night I packed my things away, getting ready to go back to Shriners Hospital the next day. The manger of the apartments kept my things in her shed till I came out of the hospital. All the things that I had stolen from me, I could have done the same back to them, but I was so angry, I didn't even think of taking something of theirs. It was just as well; it would have meant more trouble.

The next morning, May 14, 2000, I returned to Shriners Hospital to have another operation on my right leg. A friend who worked at Shriners took me. I stayed at the Hospital for more than a week.

This time, Dr. Bernsten corrected my right leg. If I didn't wear a brace I would walk on the side of my foot and that wasn't good for me to do that, according to the doctor, so he twisted my leg so I could not turn it to the side any more. He also had to move some muscles to keep the leg strong. The operation went well and it was the last operation that I had, a total of six. I was very lucky to have Dr. Bernsten, who is the assistant medical chief of staff at Shriners Hospital, for my doctor.

*Shriners Hospital* will see children from birth to age 21 years. After that they will not see you any more but, in some cases, they will help find another doctor who can continue to work with your medical conditions. Most wonderful and surprising, over their good work, is that *there is never ever any charge!*

Going to Shriners was not bad at all, because most of the kids at the hospital I already knew. When I was released, the first thing I did was pick up my paycheck and cash it. I asked Dana if I could work the next day. She said yes, but I would need a doctor's note so I took care of it.

Dana is not like any manager I have known. She is a great person to work with and she gives more chances than you should ever get. She does not act like a manager but, rather, like friend. She helps people out and works with the people instead of rejecting them. When I was hired I should have been fired the first week because of the way I treated the other employees -- very defensive and sometimes rude. For some reason I can't explain, Dana always kept me.

Since I was homeless after I was discharged from the hospital, I stayed with a friend until Jim Wilson, owner of some apartments and trailers, found me a place. He was the friend of a friend, and dealt in real estate.

The day after coming home from the hospital, I went to work with a cast on my leg and crutches to control my balance. My job was to set up the salad bar. After an hour of trying, I had to leave. My leg was killing me because I wasn't elevating it as Dr. Bernsten had instructed. I stayed off work for six months, but I still needed someplace to live. At that point, I didn't really care where I stayed as long as I didn't have another roommate.

Three days later, Jim found a place for me -- a trailer. I explained that I was not going to be able to pay rent for a while until I went back to work. He understood, and he said that everything would turn out fine. My trailer was not ready so Jan, manager of the park, put me into another one, all nice and clean. My dad helped me move my things out of storage. Jan came by often, making sure I was okay. I always replied that I was fine, as I hobbled about with my cast and two crutches.

In the weeks that followed I became friends with Cheryl, my next door neighbor, and we began talking about the Romanian culture. I don't even remember how it all started, but talking about Romania, I wanted to call them and see how everyone was doing. Cheryl allowed me to call Romania from her place and I got through. From that night on I began staying in touch with everyone at the hospital.

I began writing letters to my friends in Romania. When I got letters back from them, I asked if they would buy me some Romanian Folk Music and, sure enough, they sent three tapes. I called the house nannies a few times and they said the hospital had made a lot of changes. A school was built for kids to learn, paid for by a group of Dutch, Germans, and Americans who combined their money.

After a few months of staying in touch, I got a big idea. I began writing letters to companies and talk shows to see if they would help me return to Romania. Here is a partial list: *The Oprah Show*, many times, including at least a dozen letters sent by others; *KABC, Fox News, KCAL9 News, Jenny Jones, CBS/Los Angeles, CBS/Texas, CBS/New York, Time Magazine* and *People Magazine*.

Montel Williams' office called once to ask some questions, but never followed up.

I wrote to Maury Povich several times in a year with no response, but I did get an answer from his wife, Connie Chung, in about two weeks. She said she couldn't help me because 20/20 wasn't her show. I still have her letter.

**THE NEW CAMIN SPITAL SCHOOL**

After a year of receiving no answers and no help, I decided to write *ABC News 20/20* to request a few videotapes they had promised in the past. I also told them how I had kept in touch with the workers and the changes they had made to the hospital. I told them I planned on returning to Romania and wanted to know if they were willing to go with me and do a follow-up story on the Romanians with a new lifestyle.

At first, I never heard from 20/20, so I wrote another letter to Barbara Walters and Tom Jarriel, hoping that one of them would respond, but I never heard from them either. All I could do was to keep writing because giving up was not an option!

On Thanksgiving Day, my parents took me to our grandparents' house for dinner. Later, my mom, Cari, Grandma and I took a walk and Mom asked if 20/20 had called me yet? It really surprised me.

"Why would they call?" I asked

"They called our house, looking for you."

I got the number and, the next day, I called 20/20 to see what they wanted from me. The lady who answered knew who I was before I even said my name. Her name was Ruth Reiss.

Ruth asked me so many questions that I knew something was up. I told her that I was not going to Romania after all.

"Why not?"

"My fundraising efforts didn't work out."

"Izidor, how would you feel if we paid for your trip to Romania?"

I could not believe they would pay for my trip. I hadn't asked for a trip when I wrote to them, but I took the offer with thanks. Afterwards, I called everyone I knew to tell them I was going to Romania. I was so happy; I was going back to see my homeland and my friends.

Ruth and I stayed in touch just about every day until our trip. I even called Romania and told them I was coming back for a visit. They were very happy to hear that. Once Ruth said they were going to pay for my trip, I decided not to pay rent that month and, instead, bought twenty rolls of film and some nice clothes to wear there. I still had one problem. I did not have a camera for my film!

I had decided to use my income tax refund check. Then I learned that one of my friends had one to sell. Having learned some hard lessons about money, I checked his camera out and took pictures with it right away. Sure enough, it was a great camera so I bought it for $225.

One day during a phone conversation I asked Ruth who was going to Romania with us from the 20/20.

"Janice Tomlin and Tom Jarriel and a few doctors we're taking with us."

I knew Janice Tomlin from the first story she had done on us kids. Tom Jarriel, I knew since 1989 when I was in the hospital in Romania, but I didn't think he'd remember me.

It was decided that March 25, 2001, was the day I would leave for Romania and meet the 20/20 crew at the *Bucharest* airport. The crew left a week before me, to start their stories in *Constanta, Bucharest*, and other cities where I was not familiar. In the meantime, I called Bobbie at the hospital and told her we were coming within a week.

"Izidor, do you know they found your parents?"

I told her I did not.

"Maybe they didn't want you to know and I wasn't supposed to tell you. Don't say anything to them. I'll get in trouble."

On March 17, 2001, my family gave me a going-away party. I wasn't sure if I was coming back to the United States. Many of my friends thought I would never return. After all, I did talk about going back and staying there forever.

On March 24, 2001, I stayed at my parents' home. That afternoon, my dad took me to the store to get gifts for my Romanian friends. Next morning I woke up earlier than the rest of my family to finish packing. One by one, the rest of the family got up and by nine o'clock we were on our way. At the airport we met with the local camera crew that *ABC News 20/20* had scheduled to videotape me saying good-bye to my family.

As we walked into the airport, the news crew saw us and started taping. I tried to act as if they weren't there. I checked in and waited for the plane to arrive. Since we were early, I went for a walk with my sister Cari to get away from the camera. Before we went back inside, I smoked a cigarette and looked around, thinking in my mind that I may decide to stay in Romania if I liked it there and I wanted to remember America.

I thought back to the day I had arrived. How excited I had been to see everything at once. How challenging it was not to know the language or be able to communicate, but how happy I was to finally realize my dream of coming to America. Now I was leaving, returning to my homeland, perhaps never to return. It was a bittersweet moment in my life.

We went back inside to say good bye to my family. Jo, one of the newscasters, asked me questions abut my trip. At that point, I think my family believed I wasn't coming back. They cried. I tried not to cry, but it was too hard to hold in. I asked Jo if she could turn the microphone off and let me say good bye to my family without being on camera. They couldn't stop, so I just pretended that they weren't there. I pulled out my wallet and showed my family two pictures I'd carry with me in case I did decide to stay in Romania.

"In case I do decide to stay there, I will have something to remember you by." I walked through the gate and looked behind to see them for the last time.

Walking with me, Jo said, "Izidor, why are you going back to Romania?"

"To see my family and my friends. Plus, I want to see what Romania looks like after ten years."

"I hear that you might want to stay in Romania."

"If I can find a job while I am there, then, yes, I plan on living in Romania."

"How do you feel about finding your family after all these years?"

"I am excited to find them, and I will ask them many questions about why I was put in the hospital for all those years."

After Jo was done interviewing me, she stayed with me until I got on the plane. During the flight I tried to sleep but I could not. Around noon, we landed in *Munich, Germany*, to change planes. I went to get checked in and find out the gate number. There was a long wait in line but by three o'clock I got on board. After a stop in *Sibiu*, we headed straight to *Bucharest*.

~~~~~~~~~~~~~~~~~~~~~~~~~~~~~~

## Chapter Twenty-five

### Welcome back to Romania

I was so excited to land in Romania. Once I deplaned, I went to get all my bags together before someone could steal my things. I had heard that a lot of people steal luggage in the *Bucharest Airport*. With bags in hand, I saw a girl holding a sign: *ABC News 20/20*. For awhile I had forgotten I'd actually come with the 20/20 crew.

The girl marched up to me. "Are you Izidor?"

"Yes, I am Izidor. And you are?" The girl was angry because I had not instantly seen her holding the sign. "Where are Ruth and Janice?"

"They are waiting for you outside."

"Ruth did not tell me you were going to wait for me. Ruth was supposed to be here."

"Well, I'm the one," she replied as she helped me with my bags.

When the doors opened and we walked outside, all you could see was lights and the camera crew. I did not care whether I was being taped or not, but I was not going to let someone start yelling at me on my first arrival back to Romania. I went up to Tom Jarriel and asked him the name of that girl.

"Her name is Alina," Tom replied.

"I don't like her already, because her attitude is rude."

"We have all been waiting for you for hours and Alina is really tired," he explained. "She has been doing a lot of work for us."

After Tom told me that, I felt bad for yelling back at Alina.

So many people had been waiting for my arrival: Ruth Reiss, co-producer; Janice Tomlin, main producer and in charge of the whole trip; Tom Jarriel, reporter; Bruce, cameraman; Tom, sound man; Liviu, Romanian translator, who helps families reunite; Alina, Romanian translator, organizer, and planner of activities for our travel; and Titi, our driver. After they were done videotaping me, everyone introduced themselves.

Ruth waited for us at the *Intercontinental Hotel* in Bucharest. After twenty minutes of talking, we headed to the hotel. As we passed through the city, I was so filled with joy to see again the beauty of Romania. At that point, I wanted to stay forever.

When we got to the hotel, I met Ruth there. I had asked Janice if I could have a room with a good view so I could take pictures. I was put on the seventeenth floor with the best view that they had. Now that I was in Romania, I couldn't wait to see my family and friends.

Later, after Janice, Liviu, and I had dinner, I said goodnight. I went up in my room and looked out the balcony at my beautiful country. After a nice warm shower I slept till morning.

I dressed up in my nice clothes and wore a tie. After breakfast I went out to take some pictures and look around the city before we left for *Maramures*. By nine o'clock we went by two helicopters to *Maramures*. If we had driven there, it would have taken us fourteen hours to get to *Sighetu Marmatiei* but, with the helicopters, it only took us about five hours. For your information: *Maramures* is the county and *Sighetu Marmatiei* is the city.

**THE VIEW BY HELICOPTER**

We had a hard time finding the *Camin Spital* because of so many apartments that were now built around it, but as soon as the workers heard the helicopter, they all came out to see. We landed in a nearby soccer field. I laughed at the expressions on their faces because I had kept my word -- I returned in a helicopter!

Two men who worked at the *Camin Spital* came to greet us. They wanted to take me to the hospital so everyone else could see me. Janice said we'd wait for Ruth and Tom to land before we went anywhere. Twenty minutes later, the second helicopter landed and we boarded two vans: one, filled with the camera equipment, and the other one, filled with us.

When we got to the hospital, there were more people than I could say. We drove around the orphanage and parked the vans right in front of the school. Janice wanted me to stay in the van while Bruce got his camera ready. As I stepped out, I walked towards the house nannies and hugged them and all the kids. One of the first people to greet me there was the director. I did not know her, but she said she knew about me very well from Bobbie.

Each person that I hugged, I said their first and last name. They were surprised because they thought I had forgotten them. I did not know everyone because there were some new house nannies. After I was done hugging everyone, I went inside the school. There, the children had arranged a special program for my arrival. Afterwards, the house nannies served me food, juice, and cake, but because I was so excited to see everyone, I could not eat.

I started taking pictures of everyone. I even got to see house nannies Emilia, Dina, Florica, Marina, Dana, Olga and Marika.

"Where are Onisa and Ildi?" I wondered.

"Onisa is at home and Ildi moved to Hungary," said Bobbie.

I was really hoping to see Ildi. Emilia asked when I was going to *Casa De Batrani* (Home of the Old Man).

"After I get to see the children," I said.

"You have to go soon because the director is going to leave."

We went on the floors where I used to live ten years ago.

"Izidor, where did you sleep?" Tom asked me.

I showed him where I slept.

"Izidor, now that you are back here, have you seen the people that used to abuse you?"

"Yes, I have seen them and some are standing right in front of me as we talk."

"How do you feel about seeing them after what they have done to you?" Tom asked.

"I have learned to forgive them for their mistakes. I cannot go on hating them for the rest of my life. I am not one of those people who does not forgive easily."

Then I saw Calin and I felt bad for him because his head was bruised up. I asked Calin if he remembered who I was, and he nodded. "Calin, do you remember Marlys?"

"Yes, I remember Marlys," he replied, with a smile on his face.

After we were done in that room we went to the paralyzed room. It was still the saddest place in the world. Here, there were children who lived in their beds and did nothing but exist.

Then it was time to leave. When we got to *Casa De Batrani*, I had to wait in an office until Janice was done videotaping Cardos and Anita. Ten minutes later I went upstairs into Anita's room and we hugged for a long time, then I spoke to her and Cardos.

ANITA AND CARDOS - 2001

"Janice, can you please close the door behind you?" I asked her. "I don't want the house nannies to hear what we say."

My first question was how they liked living there at *Casa De Batrani*.

"I don't like living here," said Anita. "They don't treat us good and the food is worse than at the *Camin Spital*."

"Do the house nannies beat you here?"

"They still beat us when we don't do what they want us to do."

Hearing it made me angry. They told me that Felicia got transferred here because she was so abusive with the children at the hospital. Cardos told me she had hit him, but this time Cardos slapped her back across the cheek and told the director. The director moved her and now she works in the same building, but with the seniors. If she ever hurts anyone else, she will be fired.

After I was done speaking with Anita and Cardos, we went to see the rest of the children who waited to see me in the activity center, where they had a special program for my arrival. I noticed that all the children loved Dr. Melinda, the home's doctor. Soon Janice said it was time for us to return to the hotel.

ONISA - 2001

That night, I wanted to call Onisa to see if I could stay with her, but somehow I had forgotten her telephone number. We called the hospital and Anita, a nanny who answered, said she would take us to her home. Liviu and I drove to the hospital and picked up Anita and soon we arrived at Onisa's apartment.

When Onisa opened her door she was so surprised to see me that she cried and hugged me. I cried too… with happiness. She did not even know I was back. She was glad to have me stay and we talked a long time about my life in America. That night, I slept in her guest room. Tomorrow would be a big day. Liviu was going to take me to *Tasnad* to see my family.

I slept really well that night. For the first time in many months I felt at peace. Liviu arrived on time and we returned to the Hotel because Tom Jarriel wanted to interview me before we left.

"How do you feel about meeting your family after twenty years?"

"I am very excited to meet them and I hope that they are just as excited to see me."

"What are you going to say to your parents?"

"I don't know, but I'm sure I have a lot of questions about my history."

After we were done with the interview, I told Ruth and Janice that I needed to get some gifts for my family. In the Romanian culture, anytime you visit someone's house it was always nice to bring them a gift. Alina, Ruth, and I did the shopping. For my mother, I got coffee and flowers. For my three sisters, I bought three large boxes of chocolates. For my dad, I got a shaving cream set and the same for my older brother. All the gifts were paid for by *ABC News 20/20* and I thanked them for their kindness.

Then we headed to *Tasnad*, a six-hour drive. It was a cold, snowy day and my feet started hurting. Cold always caused pain because of the Polio I'd had as a baby. As we got closer to *Tasnad* my heart started beating faster and faster because I was a little scared about meeting my birth family for the first time since those few moments when I was eleven

"Liviu, where do we turn now?" asked Janice.

"Turn left, and the house is on your left."

I looked around at the barren surroundings. "Why are they so far away from the city?" No one had an answer.

"Do you see any one coming out, Izidor?" asked Tom Jarriel.

I gazed at the door of the hut as it slowly opened. "Yes, I see someone is coming."

Tom opened the van door for me, then patted me on my shoulder. "You're on your own now, Izidor. Good luck!"

~~~~~~~~~~~~~~~~~~~~~~~~~~~~~~~

## Chapter Twenty-six

## My Romanian Family

When I saw where they were living, it shocked me, so far away from the city. My father came out of the house to greet us. My mother followed, then my two sisters. My mother cried when she saw me, but instead of hugging them, I walked right past, to the house because I suddenly felt very hurt and angry.

I was not so sure I wanted them to touch me but, my sister, Maria, grabbed me and gave me a big hug. We went inside the house because it was really very cold. When we got settled, I got right to it and asked my parents about my past.

"Maria and Izidor, why was I put in the hospital and you never came back for me?" I asked my parents.

"You were six weeks old when you got sick," said Maria, who appeared to be the one in the family with the energy and who liked being the leader. "We took you to the doctor to see what was wrong with you. A few weeks later, your grandma and grandpa went to the hospital to bring you back home to us, but when you came home there was something wrong with your right leg." She looked at me and big tears filled her eyes.

"We went back to find out what was wrong with your leg and were told you and forty other children were infected with a disease we didn't know about. We asked the doctor to fix your leg, but the doctor would not help anymore. We had to take you to another hospital to see the doctors. That first place could not help you so we took you to another place in *Sighetu Marmatiei*, and that's where we left you. When we went back for you, you were already placed into a different hospital because nobody could help you."

The information Maria provided was similar to what Dr. Bernsten had told me about the polio virus. But to hear it from my birth mother, overwhelmed me. If she was telling the truth, I was born whole. I looked at her eyes to measure her honesty. "You mean to tell me that I was never born with a disability?"

"No, Izidor, you were born normal," she said.

"Why did you not come to see me while I was in the hospital once in a while?"

"Mugurel and your sisters were sick many times and we move around a lot, trying to find jobs to take better care of the family."

I was incredulous. "For eleven years you couldn't come to see me? There were many house nannies who asked me, 'Izidor, where are your parents?' I told them I did not have parents; they were dead. What was I supposed to say?"

I had to breathe a little before I went on because a lifetime of emotions rising up like a suddenly angry active volcano threatened to choke me. "All my life, I grew up thinking I never had any family. Maria and Izidor, do you know what it was like living in the *Camin Spital*? It was like living in hell, being abused, eating awful food, and we were treated like we were wild animals."

My parents seemed surprised to hear what I went through. Had they visited me they might have seen what I experienced, if they'd touched the scars or bruises on my body after a beating. The few parents I'd met at the hospital seemed easy to fool when the nannies told them their child had fallen or fought with another kid. It was a believable story and parents never knew the real side of the story or know how much their children were suffering. Or perhaps they didn't want to know.

"Izidor, we are sorry for what happened to you," said my mother with pleading eyes as she held her hands as if in prayer.

"I am not blaming you for what you did," I said, looking at my surroundings as I sat on the one decent stool in the house, a house that was two small rooms, a general room and kitchen, with two cots in each room. They had no plumbing and, of course, no running water; water had to be carried from a hand pump 100 yards away. The heat came from a small stove, also used for cooking. My father, my namesake, told me he chopped the wood by hand to feed the fire.

"To tell you the truth, I'm glad I was there, because if I were never there I would not have had the opportunity to go to America."

Maria leaned forward with interest. "Izidor, why did your American parents take you out without asking us?"

"Because they couldn't find you," I answered bluntly. "My American mom looked everywhere for you. She even paid the *Satu Mare* Police to search for you, but they said you disappeared once you got out of jail, and they could not find you."

I tried to understand her expression and failed. "My American mom had to go to court in order for me to get out of Romania. You were supposed to be there." I glared at my mother.

"We never heard about the trial," said Maria.

"That's a lie," I declared. "The Romanian court had it in the newspaper, on radio, and the local news. You were given more than fifteen chances to show up in court and you never did. If you were there, the Judge would have gone with your ruling." They seemed to have no reply to that information.

"Does your American family hurt you?"

I seethed at the question. "They have never hurt me."

"Did they teach you how to beg on the streets?" To her it seemed a good thing.

"No, I do not beg."

I showed them the brace I wear on my right leg. When my mother saw it she felt my leg, then broke into big tears, even more than she did when I arrived at their house. My leg was freezing cold and the brace, well, they had never seen anything like that before. It was probably not such a kind idea to show my parents the brace, but they needed to see what had happened to me. I also explained that I was going to college, working, and living on my own.

"Oh, your American parents kicked you out of the house and now you must work on the streets?"

They thought that was the only reason why I lived on my own. "In America, teenagers dream of living on their own and getting their own place." This was new information for them. In Romania, kids don't usually move out until their late thirties. Once again, I had reason to thank God I lived in America, rather than Romania.

"Izidor, after we found out you went to America, we were very angry and we went to *Baia-Mare* to find out what happened to you, said my mother. "When we asked where you were, they told us that an American family adopted you. They told us, 'Your son, Izidor Bojani, does not carry your family's name anymore. He carries the name of his new family, Ruckel."

Someone else told her that Director Viorel from the hospital sold me to the Americans. She said she heard that the Americans took children from Romania to use their body parts. Only people with little or no education would believe those rumors. Listening to her explain, it seems during the ten years I was gone from Romania, my parents thought I was dead! It was only a few weeks before I came to Romania, that Liviu found my parents and told them I was coming back to see everyone.

After we were done talking, I pulled out some pictures that my American family had made for me to take back to give to my Romanian family. As I showed them the pictures, my mother asked if she could have some. I told her my American parents sent these pictures just for them. She was surprised to get this gift from a stranger.

"Izidor, why don't you come home and live with us?" she asked.

"If I stayed, I'd need a job."

"If you live with us you'll never have to work for someone else again."

I looked around at the poor surroundings. They had so little. I had no idea how they earned enough to keep the family together. My older brother was away in another city and I suspected he might be supporting them with part of his wages earned in the mines or a factory. Did they mean it when they said I would not have to work? I wondered. Did they want to treat me like a cripple? Or perhaps they would expect me to go on the streets to beg?

I realized I judged them. Then I remembered all my mistakes and knew I should not throw the first stone, so I tried to answer kindly. "If I don't work, then I would be flustered by not doing anything, so I am going back to America because there I have more opportunities and I have a bright future."

My mom asked me how much I made a month. She tipped her head to one side and smiled. "Enough to build your Romanian family a fine house?"

I didn't want my parents to know how much I really made. My mother was already crying; I didn't want to make her cry even more. They had so little, so I lied but they were still impressed by the amount.

"Where do you work?" asked my sister, who I guessed could already be as talkative as our mother, if given the opportunity.

"I work at a restaurant and a food market," I said.

Talk of my jobs caused a jump in the conversation. "Come, we eat," said my mother.

She wanted us to eat, but I could not eat there, I felt too uncomfortable. Janice urged me to eat something my mom made for me, but I refused. Later on, I secretly felt a piece of bread that was on the table. The bread was hard, and that was another reason I didn't want to eat there.

**THE BOJANI FAMILY**
Izidor, Sr; Maria, Jr; IZIDOR RUCKEL; Maria, Sr; Onisa
Age 23    Age 21                    Age 12
not pictured: Miguel, Age 26, & Claudia, Age 25

After being at my birth parents' house for more than three hours, we said good bye, and left. The 20/20 crew stayed in a hotel in *Carei* and I was on my own for the next three weeks. I went back to *Maramures* with a driver hired by *ABC News 20/20*. The ride included a free dinner for us both on the way home. I was starving by the time we left my birth parent's house. Nicolae drove me back to *Sighetu Marmatiei*, and we got dinner at *Perla Sigheteana*, a restaurant two blocks from the hospital. I got back to Onisa's house before dawn. I was so tired and drained of emotions that all I wanted to do was sleep.

The next day I went to see if Marika was home, and she was already outside doing some work when I got there. Ildi Strimbei was with her. I was so surprised and delighted to see Ildi. "What are you doing in *Maramures*," I asked. "I thought you moved to Hungary."

"I never moved to Hungary," said Ildi. "That's a different Ildi."

She asked if I would come to her daughter's birthday party the next day? I told her I was already going to Marika's daughter's birthday's party. Marika laughed and said I could go to both.

Saturday afternoon I went to the first party and took pictures for Marika. I didn't get her daughter a birthday gift, so I gave Marika 50 Mei to give to Carmen. (That was about two dollars in American money.)

**ILDI and MARIKA 2001**

After that, I went to the next birthday party, which was for Diana, daughter of Ildi. I knocked at the door and when Diana answered, I couldn't believe how she'd grown up! I have to admit she looked very beautiful, dressed in her best outfit, looking far different than the last time we'd played as children and I'd pulled her pigtails and made her scream with my ferocious faces. Ildi brought out the cake and I took pictures of Diana blowing out her eighteen candles, then I just kept gazing at her beauty.

I was offered plum brandy wine, beer or regular wine. I tried the *Palinka* (plum brandy wine) but could not handle the taste. It's the strongest alcohol in Romania. *Palinka* is stronger than *Vodka* and whiskey put together. I enjoyed a beer or two and some wine while we played Romanian folk music and everyone danced and sang. It was a great party and I was happy to be with my old friends, especially little Diana, all grown and truly a goddess in my eyes.

Two days later, I returned to the hospital to see the house nannies and the children. When I walked in, Tibi told me he had cried the night before.

"Tibi, why did you cry?"

"Because I know you are going back to America and I am going to miss you."

I told him I would come back someday and I would see him again. He followed me to all the floors as I visited the children. Before I left, I asked the director if I could come here anytime I wanted. She said I could come as I pleased.

From there I went to the Old Man's Home to see Cardos and Anita. When I arrived, Anita, Cardos, and many other children were in school, but Dr. Melinda was always glad I came to see the children. She always made coffee and we'd smoked and drink coffee. Cardos and Anita were very surprised to see me smoke.

The doctor and the director both spoke very good English. The director is Dr. Melinda's husband and I think they make a good team. I asked him if he would allow me to take Anita and Cardos to get something to eat? "I was planning on also taking Tibi with us."

"It is fine with me," he said.

I took my friends to a nearby store to get whatever they wanted. I got them cake, juice, and bananas. I was glad that Anita was finally eating something. She seemed to come alive and a bright smile appeared on her face. Anita always worried me because she did not eat very much. All three of the kids were filled with joy and you could see it right through their eyes. After they were done eating, I took them back, then headed home myself.

Diana, the beautiful birthday girl, and her brother, Ryan, were home for Easter vacation so we could hang out together. The first few days, we all went to the hospital and the old men's home. Most of the house nannies knew them because Ildi and their father worked there. Most of the time when I went to *Casa De Batrani*, I brought Tibi with me because he liked seeing Cardos and Anita. I also took Cardos and Anita to the hospital to see the special house nannies they missed. I knew they wanted to return to the hospital to live there.

Every day, I went to see the children at both institutions and visited three to four hours at each place. Sometimes I had Diana help me translate because it was hard for me to understand everything they said, but if someone spoke to me slowly, I understood it much better.

**Tibi, Anita, Izidor, Cardos, Nanny Madalina**

Most of the time when I went places with Cardos and Anita, Tibi came, too. I never wanted him to be left out. If we went somewhere, I always made sure Tibi got to go with us. I had grown up with him and he depended on me to take him places when I took Anita and Cardos. Both directors allowed me to come as I pleased and let me take Anita, Cardos and Tibi anywhere I wanted, just as long I returned them on time.

The next day when I went to the hospital, Bobbie told me Maria, my mother, called and said she would come to *Maramures* to pick me up for Easter on the eleventh of April. She left no telephone number so I didn't know how I was going to tell her not to come here because I was going there on the 12th. Bobbie tried to call the post office to go tell them, but my parents did not have an address so I knew I had to make a reservation to put them in a hotel.

One the appointed day, my parents were supposed to come to the hospital near noon to wait for me. I still had plenty of time so I went to Diana's house for awhile to listen to an hour of folk music. I loved hearing every moment of it.

A knock came at the door. A messenger told me, "Your mother has been waiting for hours."

I told Diana that we needed to go now. When we got to the hospital, she and her brother visited friends and I went to see Maria, my mother, and Maria, my sister.

They both rushed to my side. "Izidor, did you not get my message?"

"Yes, I got it, but no, we're not leaving today," I told her. "It will be too late to travel that distance. I made a reservation at the hotel."

"Izidor, we don't stay in hotels."

"Unless you want to go home tonight alone, you'll stay because I'm not going till tomorrow morning."

So my mother decided to check out the hotel. On the way I had to keep telling my sister to stop begging. That was no way to live when one could get a job and earn a living. Suddenly a question popped into my head and I stopped walking.

"If you and my American family had met and they had asked you if you would let me go to America, what would you have told them?"

"I would have told them no, you could not have my son."

"What if it was only for medical treatment?"

"Then I might consider it. We'd have to talk about it. I would miss you so. They would have to understand how much I would miss you, how difficult it would be to let you go."

I discovered I could read between the lines of her answer. "I'm so glad you and my American family never met."

"Why are you glad for that?"

"Because now I know that you would have never let me go to America to have a better life." The thought of never having the opportunity made me feel very grateful that I had.

When we got to the hotel, I asked for the rooms, but they told me they were waiting on another reservation for the rooms. That was the last straw! I lost my temper with the lady and I started yelling at her.

"My mother and sister have not slept in two days and they have not eaten since yesterday. I have American money and I will pay extra. Just give them a place for the night only." I was so angry that I had Diana translate for me in Romanian.

"Okay, okay, they can stay."

I apologized to the lady for yelling. I told her that if my family needed anything to eat or drink, to let them get it without paying. "I will be back in the morning and you will be paid by me." She agreed.

My friends and I left the hotel to buy some supplies. When we returned I took my mother outside to talk. "I don't want you to look at me as if I am disabled, but rather as a son who is working and going to school. I want you to stop saying, 'Poor thing.' I hate it when someone pities me. It makes me feel like I'm back in the hospital."

She said she would try to remember. "Izidor, when you were at my house with the camera crew, the lady who had on the red coat pulled me to the side and gave me $1,000 Mei." In American money, it was worth thirty-seven dollars.

I thought that was very nice of the people. "There's something else I want to say. If I am going to buy you a house, I will buy it here in *Maramures*. I don't know if you like that idea, but that's where I am going to buy you a house, only in *Maramures*."

She said we could talk about it later. I gave up then, and went home to make arrangements for traveling the next day. There was a lot of confusion with drivers and changed prices, and then bus schedules and travel time so my host Ildi woke me at dawn for the trip to *Tasnad*.

"Are you going to come back and spend Easter here with us?" she asked.

"I'll be back, don't worry." I really wanted to spend Easter there in *Maramures* with all my friends, but I didn't think it would be possible.

I picked up my mother and sister and the trip began. It seemed to take forever to get to *Tasnad*. First, came a long bus ride to the train station, after waiting two hours for them to begin their schedule. Then came a seven-hour train ride to *Carei*, with stops along the way. From there I thought we were waiting for another bus until I saw Maria hitchhiking! I knew I would have a hard time getting back to my friends. At that point, I prayed that God would send a bus.

All of a sudden, out of nowhere, a bus appeared and stopped in front of me. The door opened and the driver called, "Can I give you a lift?"

"Where you are heading?" I asked.

"I'm heading to *Tasnad*."

Right then, I knew that God was there, helping me. "Thank you, Lord, for helping me get there."

When I saw my sister hitchhiking, I was not planning on staying in *Tasnad* another day. I was afraid that somehow I was going to end up being stuck there. I had to make an excuse to get back to *Maramures* quickly. Finally, we got home safely.

This time, I got to meet the sister I did not meet on my first visit. Her name was Claudia. My brother, Mugurel, was still not home. My parents said they had sent him a telegram saying I was back, but he must never have gotten it. I was really upset because I knew I would probably not meet him, man to man, during my whole time in Romania. Later, my mother visited the grave of my grandmother, who had passed away a week before I arrived in Romania. My family kept telling me I needed to rest.

"Why do I need to rest?"

"Because your leg hurts and you must be tired coming from *Sighetu Marmatiei*."

*Pity again!* "I know when I am tired and when I need to rest. Right now, I am just fine."

The whole day at my parents, I waited for Mugurel to come. I didn't expect him to make it home, but in my heart I still hoped.

Claudia told me Mugurel has a tape called L.A. and he has a song from that tape that he dedicated to me. "Mugurel doesn't even let us touch it in case we break the tape."

The song that Mugurel dedicated to me is called *"Fratele Meu,"* ("My Brother"). Here are a few words of the song that this group sings in Romanian.

## Fratele Meu (My Brother)

I have not forgotten you if you are far, I pray every night,
I pray to God that he will return my brother.
I haven't forgotten you my brother, although you are far
And know that I think about you every night.
I hear things about you and no one seems to understand me.
You are far away from me and it's hard for me,
Hey, lady, take care of my brother.
Make sure that he doesn't get hurt and he does not get sick.

When Claudia told me that my brother had a song that he dedicated to me, I went out and bought the tape to hear it for myself. The song was hard to listen to because it was sad and it showed me that he really cared.

That night, my aunt came to see me. She was surprised that I had come back to Romania. Most of the questions she asked me were about my life in America. "Izidor, why don't you come and stay the night with us," she said, "and in the morning we can take you to the city to meet with the rest of the family."

Before I could reply, my mother told her I had come here to see them so my aunt left, saying everyone would see me tomorrow.

It was another nightmare getting back to Maramures. I thought we were waiting for a bus, then discovered Maria, hitchhiking again. We waited a long time. Finally someone picked us up and we went to the city of Tasnad to meet the whole family.

The plan was to meet at the bus station. When we arrived, more than twenty members greeted me. We were only together for a short period of time because I still had a long way to go to return to my friends. Suddenly, a hush fell over the crowd as they looked up the hill. There, astride an old horse, rode an ancient man.

My mother came to my side as the old man approached. "This is my father, Izidor," she said, her voice filled with great respect. "I want you to greet your grandfather, leader of our tribe."

He barely made a motion with his head and two men lifted me to sit behind him, then slowly, he and I rode the horse one time around the bus station. He didn't say much, but I felt a certain bonding between us and his decision to take me up behind him appeared to be a mark of honor for me. Soon it was time to go.

My mother stayed with the family, but Maria and I got a ride back to *Carei*, where I would catch the bus back to *Maramures*. A guy told me he'd drive me there.

"No, thanks. I'm waiting for the bus, which comes by at 2:45."

"That bus won't be by until 5:45."

I thought he was lying.

"Izidor, we can go back home and come back at 3:00," said Maria.

"Oh, no, we are not going back home.' I again feared I would be stuck there forever. I felt the same type panic I experienced when I could not leave the hospital for America. "We are going to wait here until the bus gets here."

"What if the bus does not come here?"

"You can go home if you want to, but I am going to sleep right here until I get back to *Maramures*."

After I cooled down, we got something to eat and drink and then talked. While we sat on the hillside, I had one question I wanted to ask my sister. "Maria, if you had a son and he was disabled, would you put him in a hospital or orphanage?"

"I don't know what I would do."

"Well, let me tell you one thing. If you ever have a son or daughter and that child has some kind of disability and you put him or her in a hospital or orphanage, I will never speak to you ever again. I will never see you again."

"Oh, no, I would never put my child in a place like that." Maria was 22 years old and was at an age where she was able to get married.

"I never want my niece or nephew to be in a hospital or orphanage and go through the hell I did for all those years."

Near nightfall another guy needed one more passenger going to Maramures

"How much are you charging me?"

"One thousand Mei."

Before I could respond, Maria would not let me go with the stranger. I started getting angry again. "I will never come back here with a bus. If I ever come back, I'll hire a driver to bring me to your house and take me back that same day." How could I make her understand? "Maria, I am afraid I'm going to get stuck here."

When the bus finally came, five hours later, I got on board. Maria told the bus driver to make sure that he did not lose me. "He's not from here. He's from America."

I apologized to Maria for yelling at her. She understood me and waved good-bye. I knew that was probably going to be my last time I'd see my family for a long time.

On the bus, I looked outside, knowing I would probably never return to *Tasnad*. I had only two weeks left before my return to the United States, but it seemed that it was going by very quickly.

We stopped in *Satu Mare* to take a ten-minute break. When I returned to the bus, I went in the back way. The driver stood up. "Where is the American boy with the camera?"

I did not hear him the first time.

The whole bus asked, "Where is the American boy with the camera?"

"I'm here," I answered, sheepishly.

The driver grinned. "Okay. Just making sure we didn't leave you behind."

I got back to *Maramures* that night and got dropped off right in front of the hospital. Since the bus driver looked out for me I gave him ten dollars, in American dollars. I think he appreciated the large tip. I was never in my life so happy to be back.

## Chapter Twenty-seven

### Easter

I went home to see if Liviu, the videographer with the crew, had called me yet. Onisa said that he had and he wanted me to meet him at *Perla Hotel*. I walked to the hotel and got his room number from the desk. When I got to his room, Liviu showed me how to use a video camera that belonged to the ABC 20/20 company. They wanted me to videotape what really went on in the hospital. When the crew was there, things were very nice and cleaned up, but once they left, things were quite different.

The house nannies did not treat the children as well as they would have if the Americans were there. They knew that I knew how things really went. The staff wouldn't change things just because I was there. Since Liviu could not come to the hospital with me, he gave me the camera to use for a week.

When I got home, Ruth called to ask if I'd received the camera?

I told her I would videotape for them on one condition. "If you let me use two of your tapes to video whatever I want for my own use, then I'll do it."

"I don't think that is going to be a problem."

"I need to know for sure," I said.

"Deal done, then."

The next day, Easter, I took the camera with me when I went to see Diana. Everyone who saw it asked where I got it. I told them my American parents sent it to me through the Western Union. Everyone fell for it.

The one thing I had to do was ask the director for permission in order for me to videotape the hospital, and I got it.

Back at home, Ildi asked, "Izidor, do you want to go to church with us?"

"Why are we going to church so late at night?"

"Tonight at midnight is going to be Easter. Hundreds of people will be there."

I accepted. Long before midnight we all dressed nicely and went to church. I decided to bring the video camera with me. When we got there, I could not believe how many people were there. Such a big crowd! Ryan and I decided to video the ceremony. Most of the people had a filled basket, waiting for the priest to bless their food. The service lasted from midnight till 3:00 in the morning. I saw many people I knew from childhood or people I had met during this visit. At the end of the Mass, the priest went to the door of the church and blessed the food. I taped it all.

After we got back to Ildi's home, we looked at the tape to see how it turned out. At four o'clock I went home to sleep. The week before, Onisa gave me the key to her daughter's apartment because she was living in America. In the morning, Diana, Ryan and I went to the hospital to see the children. When we arrived, they were ready to go to the chapel built right in the front entrance. The children seemed to love going to church and invited me to come, but I had other plans.

I want to visit nanny Marika. We talked about Maria, the nanny I loved, who had died many years ago from being electrocuted.

"Marika, do you remember Maria Petreus?"

"Yes, I knew her very well, we used to spend lots of time together at her place, and sometimes she'd visit here. I still think about her and miss her very much."

"Exactly how did she die?" I asked.

"She was electrocuted at home, when she was trying to heat up some water for her coffee. It was very sad."

"So she had died by electrocution, but at home, not at work."

"Her daughter Rodica was only twelve years old when her mother died. She's been working for twelve years at the *Camin Spital*.

"Yes, I know Rodica. I met her before I ever left for America."

Marika and I decided we'd visit her grave, but we never went before I had to leave.

I spent the rest of the day visiting from one friend's home to another. I thought I would soon burst if I ate or drank another thing. This was quite a celebration. In Romania, Easter goes on for three days.

On the second day of Easter I spent the day visiting more friends. I ended up at Anti's house and our other friends soon followed. After dinner we drank and sang and danced. I should have gone home earlier because, by midnight I was drunk and couldn't even walk home. I didn't want Onisa or anyone else to see me drunk so Marius took me back to his house. I was some house guest; all night long I kept throwing up.

In the morning I was still hung over, but I went home, took a long, hot shower and went to sleep. At three in the afternoon a knock on the door woke me. It was Ryan and his father, Laci, wanting me to join them spraying girls with perfume.

Another Romanian tradition: On the third day of Easter, all the guys go to the girls' houses to spray them with perfume!

Later on that evening I went to see Diana and the family. When she opened the door I knew I was in trouble.

"Izidor, what happened? I waited for you until one in the morning. You said you'd stop by."

"I forgot, Diana, I'm sorry. I was completely drunk last night," I confessed, "and I didn't want you to see me like that."

At the doorway I heard Ildi chuckle. "I wish you would have come over last night, so we could see how you look when you're drunk. Were you funny?"

I groaned, and they laughed. "All night I thought I was going to die."

## Chapter Twenty-eight

### Romanian Folk Music

Friday, we again visited the hospital and I took more pictures of the children and the house nannies while we were there. Then we took a taxi to the Old Men's Home. There, I spoke with Dr. Melinda about helping the children.

"Dr. Melinda, I am going to send something for the children. Will you please make sure that none of the house nannies steals from them?"

"I promise, Izidor," she said. "When I get off work or when my husband gets off work, I will put all those things in my office and no one else is allowed in the office except the director."

I believed her and I knew that I could trust her.

That was the last time I visited *Casa De Batrani*. The taxi came back and I told them to wait while I said good-bye. In my heart, I did not want to leave Romania, but because the jobs were poor and money devalued, I knew I had to return to the United States. I got into the Taxi and looked back to wave to everyone who stood at the gate.

Saturday morning, Diana and I went to a concert to watch Romanian Folk Music performances. Children competed from all over Romania. The traditional music was beautiful, and lasted for three hours. I loved it! Since I was only allowed to use two videotapes from 20/20, I had to record over the Easter service.

Sunday morning, I went to the hospital early and asked the house nannies if I could videotape the children.

"Sure, go ahead and do whatever you want."

The first room I entered was the paralyzed room. There, I videotaped children rocking back and forth, in straight jackets, and hitting their heads against their beds.

On the second floor, I was not allowed to tape because some nurse told them not to let me videotape on that floor, so I went back on the paralyzed floor. As I started taping again, a group of Dutch walked in to see the children. The doctor of the hospital asked me to translate for them. When the Dutch saw that I was able to translate, they asked me if I could go on all the floors with them. Another blessing!

"Are all the children in this hospital disabled?"

"Yes, every child has some kind of disability," I answered.

"Why are there so many children here in the hospital?"

"Because their parents either don't want them or they can't afford to take care of their children."

After I was done videotaping the hospital, I went to pick up Diana to go back for the afternoon concert, but when we got there, the concert was over.

"Diana, you told me this started at one."

"That's what the sign says."

I was so angry that I missed the second concert that I walked away from Diana.

"Izidor, please…"

"JUST LEAVE ME ALONE!" I shouted.

Soon after I found out the outdoor concert time changed because rain was in the forecast. I started walking home and Diana caught up with me.

"Izidor, I didn't know that the time changed."

"Diana, you know how much this means to me and how much I love folk music."

"Yes, I know. And I am sorry."

We left it at that and went home.

"Izidor, are you going to come and see us later?" Diana asked.

"I don't think so," I responded in an angry tone.

I took a nap when I got home and when I woke up I was ashamed of losing my temper with Diana and I went to apologize to her. When I got to her house, Ildi opened the door.

"Diana is sleeping right now, but stay here and talk with me." She sighed and shook her head. "Izidor, Diana has been crying since she came home."

I felt so bad when she told me that. "It's my fault, Ildi."

Diana woke up and joined us.

"Diana, I am so sorry for getting angry with you," I said, sadly.

Ildi shook her head again before she explained it to me. "Izidor, Diana did not cry because you got angry with her. She cried because you are leaving on Monday and she is going to miss you."

Now I got it. Diana cared!

We made up and went out to buy more folk music before I had to leave. Along the way we met Cardos and Anita so we went to the hospital to visit after all. I took more pictures and watched television with the kids. After a few hours we went to buy the folk music.

While I was in Romania, I planned on buying as much music as I could. If I had $1,000, I would have probably spent half of it on music. It cost more money to mail the tape to America than to buy it so that meant I was going home with an extra suitcase.

Every night I'd listen to my latest purchases to see if I liked the tapes. Most of them I did like, but they still weren't exactly the ones I wanted. What I kept looking for was Romanian Folk music sung traditionally by groups of singers in harmony.

After two weeks in Romania, I ran out of money. I called my parents and asked them if they would send me another $100. I told them to go to my place and get the money from there and if they could, please send it through the fastest way possible.

The next day, Diana and I took a taxi to the bank to get the money out, but there was a mix-up about the secret code numbers so it took two more days, several long-distance calls to my parents, Western Union forms and, finally, the help of Ruth at 20/20 for me to get my money. Finally, I received my $100, worth $2,700 Mein in Romanian money. I planned on spending 500 Mei in *Maramures* and the rest in *Bucharest*.

### Sunday, April 20, 2001

Sunday afternoon, I went to the hotel to see Liviu and return the camera. He'd bought several large boxes of chocolate for me to give out to the children. When we got to the hospital, the children were already in bed.

First, we went to the paralyzed room, which was on the first floor. Most children there could not eat chocolate. The whole point of giving out the chocolate was for Liviu to videotape the children.

After that, we went to the third floor, where Tibi was. There, we were not allowed to videotape, but we still gave the children the chocolate. Then, we went right across from Tibi's floor. On all the other floors where we went, we were allowed to tape as I gave out the candy.

When we completed the assignment, Liviu did an interview with me, about my feelings about the condition of the hospital and the condition of the children.

"The hospital has improved a lot." I said, "But the condition of the children has not changed. Children were still being treated as if they were less than human, worthless."

## Chapter Twenty-nine

### My last day in Maramures

Monday morning, I woke at 7:00 a.m. This was to be my last day, a day of sad good-byes. First thing I did was go to Diana's house and eat breakfast with them. An hour later, I went to Anti's for coffee. After that, I went back home to pack all my things. Liviu arrived on time.

"Izidor, are you ready to go?"

"I have not said good bye to the house nannies and the children yet."

"Okay, I'm going to get some of my money exchanged and I'll be back in an hour. Please try to be ready when I come back."

I went downstairs to say good bye to Ildi first because she had to go to work. Her son Ryan missed school my last day. Diana did not have to go to school until the afternoon. Together, we three took a taxi to the hospital.

"Can you pick us up in twenty minutes?" I asked.

"I'll just wait for you here and I am not going to charge you."

"Thank you," I said.

My friends waited while I said good bye to everyone. The first person I went to see was the director.

"Thank you for letting me come here as I pleased and for letting me videotape the children."

"Izidor, here is a box of chocolates I got for you," she said.

"You should not have done that, but thank you."

I went upstairs to tell everyone good bye as fast as I could.

We took the taxi back to Diana's place and soon Liviu arrived. As I hugged everyone and said my good byes, Liviu put my bags in the car. Everyone was crying, knowing they might never see me again. I pulled Diana aside and gave her sunglasses that my sister, Maria, gave me. She did not want to accept it.

"I don't have much to give you, but please accept this to remember me by." Then I kissed her.

She took the sunglasses and gave me a hug, crying.

I was close to tears myself. "Diana, you have to be strong. I don't want to see you cry."

She wiped her tears and we went back to the group. I had a difficult time holding back my own tears. I knew I was going to miss everyone very much and, most likely, I was never going to see them again. I got into the car, turned and waved as we drove away. I didn't hold back the tears anymore.

From *Maramures*, we headed to *Tiger Neamt* to see Marin. Marin had been living in the United States. I heard he come back to search for answers about his birth family. Somehow, his papers had a flaw of some kind and he got stuck in Romania. Next morning, when we went to see Marin, Liviu had me wait outside while he spoke with the director. Twenty minutes later, I went in.

My first question to Marin was, "What are you doing back here in Romania?"

"I came back to find out about my childhood and find my birth parents," he said. "Somehow my papers got messed up and now I can't get back to America."

He looked like he would soon cry and I remembered how sad he was when it took two whole years for John to get him out in the first place. "Izidor, I want to get out of Romania and go back to America. I want to work at a fast food restaurant like you."

I smiled at his wish. "Marin, believe me, you do not want to work in a fast food restaurant for the rest of your life."

"Izidor, do you know how I can get the paperwork in order so I can leave Romania?"

"I don't know where to get the paperwork, Marin. I'm not familiar with this town. I'm sure your friends here can help you get whatever you need."

But in Marin's confused mind, he couldn't figure out anything, all he wanted was to get the heck out of Romania.

"Marin, I have a message from your family," I said. "They said they miss you very much and that they love you very much."

"If they really loved me, then why have they not written me any letters?"

I told him I didn't know, but I believed it had been hard for his parents to let him leave. "No matter where you live or what country you are in, your parents from America are always going to love you as if you were their own son."

He couldn't believe his parents still loved him.

"Sometimes parents act as if they are okay and there isn't anything wrong with them," I said. "Some parents don't like to cry in front of their children, so they hold it in. Marin, my parents had a hard time with me. In some ways, they still do, but that never meant they didn't love me because I did something wrong."

Marin started crying then because he knew I couldn't do anything to help him get out. "Have you asked God to help you?" I asked him. "Marin, if there is anyone that can help you, it is going to be God. God made it possible for you to come to America in the first place. Maybe you were brought here to help other people that need your help. Teach people things that you have learned. The place where you're staying is very nice and the people seem to like you."

"I like the people, too, but I don't want to be here in Romania. I want to go back to America."

After I finished my interview with Marin, Liviu did one with Marin alone. When they were done, Liviu asked the director if we could take Marin out to lunch with us. She told us we had to be careful. "Marin tries to run away."

We asked Marin if he was going to run away if we took him out to lunch.

"No," he said. "I won't run away from you."

We went to an Italian restaurant close to Marin's place. There he asked me for a cigarette, and that shocked me. I never thought he would ever smoke. On the other hand, I never thought I would smoke cigarettes either. I took some pictures of Liviu and Marin before we headed back.

Liviu then did an interview with me after we left Marin. "Izidor, why is it that most children who have gotten out of the hospital seem to have problems with their families?"

I chose my words carefully. "One of the reasons is because these children are not used to living with a family that actually cares and loves them. They think it's some kind of a trick, and they wait to be beaten to get things back to what they believe is normal -- beatings and yelling."

I thought about my awesome American family. "I had a very hard time fitting in with my American family for a long time. Parents should always be prepared for the problems that they are going to have to handle. There were many parents that adopted children from Romania, who did not see the problems coming. They had no idea of the challenges they faced. It's been hard for all of them."

After my interview, we drove to Bucharest and rented a hotel room there for the night. It took us about seven hours. The next day I would return to America,

### April 25, 2001

In the morning I was ready when Liviu picked me up at ten o'clock. I spent the last few hours, gazing from my balcony, storing my last view of Romania as I listened to my beloved folk music. I blasted the volume and when I opened the door, people came out of their rooms to find the music.

From the hotel, Liviu and I went to the store to buy more folk music since I still had $50 left. I bought two CDs. and three more tapes, all of folk music, and now I was broke -- no more money.

We headed to the airport. In the car, I put on one of my tapes and by the time we got there, Liviu started liking my music. After we checked in, Liviu looked at my plane ticket.

"Izidor, I think that you missed your flight. According to this, it says your flight left at seven this morning."

Sure enough, I had missed my plane. I was not angry that I missed my flight because I still wanted to stay in Romania so bad, but I also knew I had to return to the United States. If I were able to find a job here, I would have stayed without a second thought.

Liviu called Janice in New York City, two in the morning, their time. She was upset that I had missed my flight, but said she'd get back to us. Within ten minutes, she called again.

"You've got two options, Izidor," she said. "Option one is to stay in Romania for two more days. Option two is to go to Germany and stay overnight at the airport and fly out the next afternoon. What will it be?"

In my heart, I wanted to stay in Romania the two extra days. Diana would be so surprised. But I knew Liviu would have had to stay with me and that would take him away from his own plans. "Janice, I'm going to Germany and just spend the night there."

"Izidor, I'll call the Munich airport and ask them to put you in the VIP launch," she said. "Someone will meet you at the gate when you land. Safe trip." Then she hung up.

I went to Romania with two bags, but I was leaving for America with three bags. I knew I might have a hard time getting through, but I tried it anyway. The bags were over the weight limit, which meant that I had to pay 130 American dollars. I did not have one penny to my name. Liviu thought I'd have to leave some of the things there.

"I don't think so," I declared. "These are gifts that my friends gave me and gifts to bring to my family."

The ticket agent listened as I spoke, and I began to feel frantic. "Liviu, I have all my folk music in this bag. It's my connection to my culture. I can't leave the music here, I can't."

I think that the heart of the ticket agent was touched. She seemed to sense how much it meant to take my gifts home, and I was blessed once again.

"Mr. Ruckel, it is your lucky day. We are not going to charge you for the extra bag."

I thanked her with all my heart and shook her hand for several moments for helping me get through. After I was all checked in, Liviu said good bye and left me alone. All I had to do was wait for my flight.

When I got to Munich, no one was waiting for me. No one let me use the VIP Lounge. I couldn't get through to Janice in New York, so I spent a long, lonely night, starving and wandering around the terminal. By the next afternoon I was never so happy to get out of Germany and go home.

I landed late afternoon in Los Angeles. Jo and her camera crew were waiting.

"Izidor, how was your trip coming from Munich?" she asked.

"It was fine, and I'm glad to be back home." I looked around. "Jo, where is my family?"

"Your mom will be a few minutes late. Her car broke down on the freeway, but *ABC News 20/20* paid for a limousine to pick her up."

I smiled at the thought of Mom riding alone in the back of a big limo; she deserved it. When Jo offered to buy me something to eat I never was so glad for a favor in my life. Soon after I filled my growling belly, my mom arrived and it was a tearful reunion. We went into the VIP room to do an interview. I gave Jo the six videotapes Liviu sent with me. She would forward them to Janice.

After the interview, we headed home. I stayed the night at my parents' house. We talked a lot and had a good reunion. There was so much to say, so much to tell. The next day, Mom and Jennifer took me home. I was glad to be back.

Two days later, after the jet lag, I went back to work. Nothing had changed on the outside, but everything had changed on the inside. I started looking for a second job to help my birth family in Romania but, as usual, I had a hard time. Through it all I listened to my collection of thirty cassettes and six CDs of my beloved Romanian folk music.

A few weeks later, a plan began to form in my mind. I started writing letters again to television programs and charitable organizations, asking if they were interested in helping me start an organization for the Romanian Children. Again, I got no replies but, like always, I never ever gave up.

On June 8, 2001, *ABC News 20/20* aired the show on the Romanian orphans. Called "Children For Sale," it told how parents sold their children for money and how children lived in the streets, begging to survive. There was also footage from my hospital, showing children tied up, rocking back and forth, others hitting their heads against their cribs, and still other children wearing wet and soiled clothes.

It was the truth that they showed. The story once again touched the world. But there was one story that *ABC News 20/20* did not show, the story about Marin and his struggle to get out of Romania and return to the United States.

After the program, I called my parents to see what they had thought of the show. They loved it and they were heartbroken to see that things were still much the same way as ten years ago. To be honest, I would have thought the Romanian government would have made a lot of changes after the first story that 20/20 did in 1991. Now I don't think I believe things will ever change unless help comes from outside the country. There is so much poverty, people can't even think right. After viewing the show, I was even more determined to help these children.

On Monday morning, I called Ruth, the producer of 20/20, to find out why they did not air Marin's story. She explained they had to edit because of time limitations and because they did not have enough information on Marin's story to air it.

While I had her on the phone, I asked if she could refer any organization that might help me with my dream?

"There's an organization in San Diego called *'Children Of The World.'*" She gave me their number. "Ask for Rebecca. She's the president of the group."

I thanked her and she wished me good luck. When I dialed the number, Dana, the woman who answered, said she wasn't in.

"Well, maybe you can help me," I said. "My name is Izidor Ruckel and I got your telephone number from ABC 20/20 News. I want to know if you allow people to team up with your organization?"

"It depends," she replied. "What's the Cause?"

"I'm trying to find an organization I can team with to help the Romanian orphans."

"Wait a minute! What's your name again?"

"My name is Izidor Ruckel."

"Are you the Izidor Ruckel who was on 20/20 Friday night?"

"Yes, that's me."

"Wow! I thought that story was great," said Dana. "It was awful to see those children tied up and the others, living on the streets."

"That's why I'm trying to team up with an organization like yours to help these children."

"We would love to team up with you, Izidor," she said. "I think it would be great to have someone like you in our organization. You were there; you lived through that experience. Let me call Rebecca and get back to you."

I thanked her and after I hung up, I just sat still for a moment, being grateful and thanking God for my latest blessing for the children.

Three days later, Dana called. "You're in, Izidor," she said. "Rebecca gave her okay. She says she's glad you contacted us."

With the "Children Of The World" endorsement, I called my friend Maggie for help to create a special show about the Romanian orphans. She even found business people willing to provide free space for my speeches. I prepared stories about Cardos, Anita, Marin and Duma, and Maggie booked my first public appearance on July 21, 2001.

The first appearance was disappointing; not many people showed up. I needed to do more promotion and, thinking positively, I decided I needed a bigger space to hold the crowd!

The new location would be located at the Multiplex movie theater. It cost $250 to rent the space to seat 200 people for an early morning presentation. A week before my show, the manager of the theater wanted me to get approval from 20/20 to show the tape that aired on June 8, 2001.

"No tape, no booking," he said.

I got really upset at that ultimatum. I knew I'd have little luck getting that approval in time because the media takes forever to respond to a request. Feeling overwhelmed, I asked God to help me as I typed out the letter and faxed it to 20/20. Miraculously, three days later, I got the approval I needed to show the tape at my show. Thank you, God!

I called Dana and told her I'd be doing my first big presentation. She was so excited to hear that news. "I'm flying in from Texas to see you, Izidor. I've got to witness the launch of your program."

Saturday dawned, perfect and bright. When I got to the theater early for the nine o'clock show, people were already waiting in line.

Seeing the crowd helped calm the butterflies in my stomach, not only from nerves before speaking, but because I didn't have the $250 to pay the rent on the place. I was charging a dollar to get in so I could pay off the manager. The crowd was so big, I paid him off in full.

This is how I did the presentation. First, I showed the video titled "Children For Sale," a 40-minute show. This program gave an overview of the situations among the Romanian abandoned children. After that, I personalized it with details about my friends, Cardos and Anita.

### Cardos

Cardos was born in the small town of *Baia-Mare*. He was put in the *Camin Spital* -- Home Hospital of the Irrecoverable Children -- because his parents could not afford to take care of him and because his disability, which is locking knee joints. Cardos is 23-years old and now lives in *Case De Batrani* -- Home of the Old Men.

In Romania, when a disabled orphan boy becomes eighteen, he is forced to go to the Home of the Old Men. He has no other option. As you can imagine, Cardos does not like his new home. As a man, he dreams of living independently, but Romanian law compels him to a life of institutions.

Cardos is a bright fellow and a quick learner. He would love to become publicly educated, but because of his disability he is denied access to any schools. In spite of that denial, he has taken it upon himself to learn how to read, write and play the piano with a help of a worker at the Home of the Old Men. While I was in Romania, I asked my friend what he wanted to do with his future.

"I want to find my parents and hope that they will take me out of this place," he said.

I hope, in the future, I can personally help Cardos fulfill his dream to find his parents.

### Anita

Anita is one of the many children I grew up with at the hospital. She is 22-years old now and was abandoned by her parents in her early childhood. In 1993, Anita was one of the many kids chosen to come to the United States for medical treatment, but before she could leave, her parents took her back.

After the Americans left, Anita's parents put her on the streets to beg for money. While she was at home, her parents beat her, often with a horsewhip, and she was raped by one of her family members. Workers from the hospital found Anita begging on the corner in *Baia-Mare*. They took her off the streets and now she finds herself living in the Home of the Old Men. The workers found Anita to be ill as well and began to treat her for her sickness.

Once back in the care of the government facility, Anita has not been the same. She has lost a tremendous amount of weight and barely eats her meals because she is dying of cancer. Can there be any hope for Anita? I don't know, but I am confident that she is in God's good hands.

During my visit, I had the opportunity to take Anita, Cardos, and another boy named Tibi off the hospital grounds. It was during these times that she was willing to eat and just seemed to come alive. I know the reason: during those brief moments, she felt free.

Anita recognizes that her time on Earth is limited. She has made it known that her desire is to die at a home, with someone who cares for her. She will never return to her parents' house. Is there a home for Anita? A home where she can rest in peace and know that someone is with her all the way to the end? I have known Anita for most of my life. If I could, I would choose to be with her until she goes to Heaven, for surely, Angels will take her there, to God."

# # # #

After I closed my show, many people wanted to help by donating money to the Romanian orphans. Other people wanted to speak with my parents. Luckily, my parents came to my show to answer any questions people might have for them.

Dana had arrived the night before. "I'm amazed at how well you did on your first time out. Congratulations, Izidor."

People donated the money to pay off the theater when I confessed to them that I had rented the theater, strictly on faith alone. Dana collected the other money for the Children. It pays to have faith. The next day, the theater manager came to my work and returned the rental fee.

"My boss wants you to use the money for the Romanian orphans," she said.

Another miracle!

I did a second show in Temecula, California on October 21, 2001. That turned out to be a great success, too. I was grateful for my Dad's help with the work to prepare for the presentations. How wonderful it is that our relationship is loving again. My parents always kept believing in me, even when I was acting so crazy. I am so blessed.

Dana called to say "Children of the World" provided more blessings. The organization would sponsor two shows for me. On February 23 through 27 of 2002, they flew me to Houston and Chicago to do my presentation on the Romanian orphans. The response was very positive.

## Chapter Thirty

### The End of this book is the Beginning of my work

I can see that Romania has improved from the last time I was there in 1990. The streets are much cleaner and many buildings have been repainted. Best of all, most of the orphanages and hospitals have changed for the better. I believe the change is due to the work of international charities and funds from other governments, and because the world learned the terrible secret of Romania's abandoned children.

Children are now getting an education. Those who can, are taken for walks every day. Some even receive money from the house nannies for doing chores. Chosen children continue to be taken home with the house nannies to spend a day or night with them and their families, but that is a bittersweet experience -- loving it; knowing they belong only for a day.

Some things have not changed. Children continue to wet themselves and sit all day in soiled clothing. Even I know about adult diapers or rubber pants. Mentally and emotionally ill children still hurt themselves and are abused by impatient house nannies, while others continue to rock back and forth. The nasty food continues to be a miserable excuse for nutrition, and some children often vomit after taking a few bites of their meal. I had seen, with my own eyes, a few children eat their lunch and, at the same time, throw it up. In spite of all this, every day, with the help of people from around the world, Romanian orphanages and hospitals are changing. They may not change as quickly as we would like, but they are improving every day.

House nanny Dina got married and has two children of her own. She was on leave for two years to care for her children. She still lives in the same house and continues to keep in contact with the children at the hospital.

Emilia got married as well and has two daughters. Her husband works at the old men's home where Cardos and Anita are living. Emilia and her family live with her mother until they find an apartment or a house to buy. She still works at the hospital and loves the children. I knew she would be a great mother because she was always so kind with us.

Ildi does not work at the hospital anymore because of an accident that happened to a child there. One child put a smaller child into the bathtub filled with hot water. The boy screamed and when Ildi came, she found him in the bathtub, burned. He was rushed to the hospital, but he was so severally burned, he died. Ildi and other nannies were held responsible. Three other nannies were never fired, but Ildi was fired on the spot. I don't think that it was right. She works now at a magazine store.

What happened to the boy was an accident and I'm sure it was a lesson that all the house nannies learned. When I think of the outright abuse some of them gave out to use -- the beatings, the other punishments -- those are the ones who should have been fired. *They did those cruel acts on purpose.*

Marika has worked at the hospital for over 28 years. Now she works with the babies on the second floor. She continues to live in the same apartment she did when I visited her in my early childhood, and will retire in 2006.

Florica has opened a family business that is run by her aunt. She's had three children of her own since I left the hospital.

Marina and Dana are single and have no children, but they continue to work at the hospital with the *special needs* children.

My friend Tibi is now transferred to the Old Men's Home with Anita and Cardos, since he turned 21 years old. Living there is not as bad as it seems because of Dr. Melinda, and the director of the Home, her husband. There, the children get to go out and some have more freedom than others, depending on their abilities. Cardos, Anita and Tibi are still permitted to visit the *Camin Spital* once in a while with supervision.

Janice Tomlin transferred from ABC News to CBS News. She and Tom Jarriel are the ones who have continued updates on the Romanian orphans. I don't think that anyone could have done a better job. It's nice to know people from the media who remember the ones left behind.

I have gone into detail as I shared my experience of living in The Hospital of the Irrecoverable Children, the secret Romanian dump for "misfit" humans, and now it is my desire to help other children in the Romanian orphanages, children living on the streets and in the sewers, and children living in cruel hospitals.

One of my dreams is to build a shelter there for homeless kids and kids that are abused. No child should ever have to live on the streets or beg. Children as young as ten-years old, work like slave in Romania. It was one of the things I saw; kids working when they should have been in school. No child should ever go through hell because of the mistakes of adults. The children always pay the price, not the grownups. The children don't ask to be born!

My future plan, after I complete my education, is to live in Romania and open my own business. I also would like to work in orphanages and hospitals with children who are mistreated. I *know* what they have endured. A goal can be achieved if you really work towards it and set your mind to it. In my mind, it is already done; now I only have to do the work to make it a reality -- one step at a time. I continue to stay in touch by phone and letter with the children and the house nannies at the hospital and the old men's home, including Dr. Melinda.

As for Marin Moldovan, he continues to be stuck in the old folk's home and continues to cry for help. Perhaps by my telling his story here, someone will step forward who can get him out.

John Upton, the one who all the children called Johnny, and I got back in touch to see what we could do as team to help the rest of the abandoned children. We think it may be better to help them in Romania, in their own country, by bringing supplies and specialists to them. It would also help the economy.

One of the things I would like to see, is for Cardos, Anita, Tibi and Marin to be put into a four-bedroom apartment, with a care taker to help them get around and to cook for them. I know that this type of assisted living would work because it is already happening in some places. Perhaps I can make this wish come true with profits from this book.

I leave you with these thoughts.

A new Romanian law was passed not long ago. If a parent visits their children in a hospital or an orphanage every six months, then they are not considered abandoned according to this law. I don't think I agree with this new rule. Most of these parents don't really care for their children or they would find a way to keep them in the family. To chain a child to a life of cruel abandonment is wrong, in my opinion. These biological parents can't own a child, just because they gave birth. I have learned there is a whole lot more to parenting that that! Children are not chattel, like a cow or a pig, a product that can be sold or trained to beg for money. No, children are human beings with a right to a better life.

Remember this: Your rewards are according to what you do, not by your thoughts or by your personality but, rather, by what you do, your actions and how you help others. ***Do unto others, as you would want them to do unto you.*** There is one person will always know what you do for others. . It can be hidden from the world, but not from the Almighty One.

God works through people's lives in mysterious ways and things happen for a purpose, whether we realize it or not. It is by God that we have a gifted mind to help others, who cry out, asking for help. With God's help, and yours, I will continue to work for the abandoned Children of Romania.

Thank you for purchasing my book and investing in the Children's future. If you would like to learn more about my plans I'll be glad to add you to my mailing list. Please visit my web site and leave your name and e-mail address:

http://www.izidor.org

Or, if you prefer, send your name and snail address to:

**The Izidor Ruckel Children's Fund**
**Box 515165**
**St. Louis MO 63151**

**romania@JoanBramsch.com**

Thank you very much. Together, we can make the difference.

The End... *but it's really the Beginning!*

Made in the USA
Las Vegas, NV
01 June 2022